Merry Christm♡

Reg —

from Olga + Russ

Dec 25, 1970

I do not Loan !

Ha !

PANORAMA OF WORLD ART

———

ART OF THE FAR EAST

ART OF THE

FAR EAST

Text by HUGO MUNSTERBERG

HARRY N. ABRAMS, INC. Publishers NEW YORK

For Elizabeth and Werner
who share my love for Oriental art

Front end papers:

River Landscape. Artist unknown. Ink on paper, height 16$^7/_8$″. Sung period,
twelfth century. Freer Gallery of Art, Washington, D.C.

Back end papers:

Detail of *Heiji Monogatari* scroll. Color on paper, full height 16$^3/_4$″.
Kamakura period, thirteenth century. Museum of Fine Arts, Boston

Library of Congress Catalog Card Number: 68-26866

Contents

PREFACE

This book, of which the illustrations form such a vital part, would have been impossible without the generous co-operation of the photographers who took the pictures, and the museum curators and collectors who gave permission to use their material. I wish to express my thanks to all these people, especially Mr. Usher Coolidge of the Fogg Art Museum, Mr. John Pope of the Freer Gallery of Art, Mr. Laurence Sickman of the William Rockhill Nelson Gallery of Art and Mary Atkins Museum of Fine Arts, and Mr. Earl Morse who, as on previous occasions, has kindly placed photographs at my disposal. I would also like to thank the photographers, above all Mr. Leo Spies, who took the pictures of the objects from the Munsterberg Collection, and Mr. Money Hickman and Mr. Millar Guthrie who allowed me to use their photographs of Japan.

NEW PALTZ, NEW YORK   HUGO MUNSTERBERG

Introduction

The oldest artistic traditions in the world today are those of the Far East. Others, such as those of Mesopotamia, Egypt, and Minoan Crete, have more ancient beginnings, but none of these has survived into the modern period. Only in Eastern Asia are there civilizations which can trace their origin to prehistoric times and show a continuous development through some four or five thousand years. Long before the Greeks developed a cultural identity—not to mention the peoples of contemporary Europe—China had emerged as a definite entity with its own artistic culture.

The beginnings of this process go back to the Neolithic era, when in both China and Japan, and somewhat later in Korea, a remarkable pottery culture developed, which already showed the great gift for ceramics that is an outstanding characteristic of the art of the Far East. If there is one area in which the peoples of China, Korea, and Japan have excelled over the centuries, reaching heights never surpassed and seldom equaled by any other culture, it is the creation of pottery which combines beauty of form and decoration with utility and which, especially in prehistoric times, was a major art form, giving expression to the deepest aspirations of the people.

Ting-shaped ceremonial vessel. Bronze, height $9^7/_8''$. Shang period, c. thirteenth century B.C. Collection of H.M. the King of Sweden

7

The first of these prehistoric cultures to use metal, develop a written language, and have organized urban centers was that of China under the Shang rulers, and this civilization, which evolved in the Yellow River valley almost four thousand years ago, has continued in unbroken succession down to the present day. The most remarkable creation of the Shang people was the magnificent bronze vessels, which were used as ritual objects in worshiping the forces of nature and the spirits of the dead. They represent the first great artistic achievement of the cultures of the Far East, and today they are regarded as among the finest bronzes ever produced. Jade, a stone which the Chinese have always regarded as both precious and auspicious, was the only other medium which played an important role in Shang culture, where it was used for small-scale carvings and ornaments.

The Shang dynasty, which lasted for about five centuries, was followed by the Chou, who ruled China throughout most of the first millennium. By and large, their art represents a continuation of that of the Shang people, although, as the centuries passed, there were marked changes both in the shapes of the bronze vessels and in the symbols used in their decoration. Arts such as painting and sculpture, which had previously been quite minor, now emerged as significant forms, and during the Late Chou period, from the sixth to the third century B. C., the decorative arts, especially lacquer, textiles, jewelry, and ornamental jade carving, developed a new excellence both in their mastery of techniques and in the beauty of their designs.

While China was producing the first classical statement of its ancient art, Japan and Korea continued to exist on a Neolithic level, for it was not until the end of the pre-Christian era that metal culture reached those

Seated Bodhisattva Maitreya from Lung-mên. Stone, height 14³/₈". Six Dynasties period, sixth century A.D. Rietberg Museum, Zurich. Von der Heydt Collection

◄ Rubbing of men harvesting and shooting waterfowl. Stamped tile. Han period, second century A.D. Private collection, Cheng-Tu, Szech-uan, China

countries. In Japan a new period of art arose with the advent of the Yayoi civilization, which had been brought to the Japanese islands from the continent about 200 B. C. Both the Japanese and the Koreans derived their metal culture from China, where, under the Han rulers, a great empire had arisen. This first universal state of the Far East, which included not only China proper but also northern Korea, Manchuria, parts of Central Asia, and northern Indo-China, played a role in Eastern Asia much like that of the Roman Empire during the same period in the West. Containing millions of people and boasting great cities like Ch'ang-an and Loyang, which had magnificent palaces and temples decorated with paintings and sculptures, the Han Empire, which lasted some four hundred years, represents the culmination of the early phase of Chinese art; and it is no wonder that the Chinese, even in later times, referred to themselves as the men of Han.

The next major event in the cultural history of the Far East was the introduction of Buddhism, which transformed not only the art of China but also that of Korea and Japan. Although originally an Indian religion, this faith spread throughout Eastern Asia and continued to be important in the Far East long after it had virtually died out in the country of its origin. In fact, one could well say that the next chapter in the art of this region is primarily Buddhist, for all the religious art during the first millennium after Christ was

Nyorin Kannon. Color on silk. Heian period, twelfth century. Museum of Fine Arts, Boston

created for the greater glory of the Buddha and his church. Inspired by a common religious faith and using the same Indian iconography, the Buddhist art of China, Korea, and Japan is very similar in style, showing the universal character of this art. Magnificent temples with deeply moving images and wall paintings were made throughout the Far East, reflecting the fervor of the religious faith which existed at this time. The secular art, although also on a high level, is secondary to the great religious art of this era.

With the tenth century, when European civilization was just beginning to take form, China, Japan, and Korea had reached a height of sophistication and artistic culture which has rarely been attained in the history of mankind. Under the Sung rulers in China, the Koryo dynasty in Korea, and the Heian in Japan, an aesthetic sensibility was developed, which produced some of the greatest art ever to come out of the Far East. Especially in painting and ceramics, some of the best work was created during these centuries, which correspond to the medieval period in Europe. But while the art of the Romanesque and Gothic period represented the beginning of the great achievements of Europe, that of Sung China, Koryo Korea, and Heian Japan marked the culmi-

Detail of the *Lady Wen Chi* scroll, showing a camp with horses in Mongolia. Ink and color on silk. Sung period, twelfth century. Museum of Fine Arts, Boston

Plate with floral design. Cobalt on porcelain, diameter 14⁷/₈″. Ming period, fifteenth century. Calouste Gulbenkian Foundation, Lisbon

nation of a long artistic development and, for China and Korea at least, a climax which was followed by a decline.

The single most remarkable achievement of this period is undoubtedly the landscape painting of China, which in the eyes of many critics represents the greatest school of landscape painting in the history of world art. Executed largely in ink on silk or paper and forming either a horizontal or vertical scroll, these landscapes are, in the words of the eleventh-century painter and critic Kuo Hsi, truly wonderful. Inspired by Taoist philosophy, they embody the essence of nature in a kind of artistic shorthand which gives expression to the mystery of the cosmos and the nature of the Tao, or ultimate reality. Using towering mountain peaks, gnarled trees, and misty atmosphere, the painter suggests not just the appearance but the very spirit of nature. Man, if represented at all, is reduced to a minute size, indicating how unimportant he is in the grandeur of the cosmos; and the viewer is supposed to identify himself with the tiny figure and, in this way, become one with nature.

Travelers in a Landscape. By Hiroshige. Colored woodblock. Edo period, nineteenth century. Private collection, New York

In Japan the most outstanding artistic development of these centuries was the evolution of a typically Japanese school of narrative scrolls called *Yamato-e,* or Japanese painting, in contrast to the Chinese-inspired work which had flourished earlier. Combining the narrative with the decorative, these paintings exemplify the qualities which, throughout the centuries, were to characterize the indigenous Japanese pictorial tradition. Works like the Genji scroll, illustrating Lady Murasaki's famous novel, *The Tale of Genji,* reflect this Japanese style at its very best, with its marvelous sense of decorative design and its elegance and sophistication tinged with melancholy. The same sense of beauty is also found in the religious painting of the period, such as the type of scroll where the golden figure of the Buddha appears in the sky over the green mountain landscape of Japan. These works show that Japan, although deeply indebted to the art and culture of China, developed certain strains which are truly native in character.

The other great achievement of this period is its ceramics, for in China and Korea this is the classical age of both pottery and porcelain. There is widespread agreement in the East as well as the West that Sung and Koryo ceramics are the finest ever produced: certainly for excellence of workmanship, beauty of design, and subtlety of color, Sung and Koryo porcelains have never been surpassed. When painted decorations are used, they are employed very sparingly with results that are both pleasing and filled with life. Perhaps the single most important contribution of the Far East to the visual arts is that made by the Chinese and Korean potters of the eleventh to thirteenth centuries when this art was at its height.

The philosophical and religious inspiration for some of the best of the Late Sung painting was Ch'an Buddhism, or Zen as it was called in Japan, where it had a profound influence upon the arts in subsequent centuries. Zen-inspired Chinese-style ink painting became predominant during the fifteenth century and produced some of the masterpieces of Japanese art. Not only in painting but also in landscape gardens, in architecture, and in the tea ceremony, which was so essential to the development of the crafts, Zen Buddhism was the source of much that was best in the art of Japan.

In China the later dynasties, notably the Ming and Ch'ing, brought forth a flourishing school of crafts, especially porcelains, as well as a large and significant output of painting. It was these later Chinese porcelains with their pure white bodies and beautiful decorations executed in cobalt blue or bright enamel colors which first aroused the enthusiasm of the West for the art of the East, and which had such a profound influence upon European ceramics. Although the painting of the Ming and Ch'ing falls short of the level attained by the Sung, the Chinese themselves have always greatly admired the best of these later artists, a taste which Western critics are beginning to share.

In Japan the art of the seventeenth century, which includes the later part of the Momoyama and the early part of the Edo period, is rightly considered one of the high points in the history of Japanese art. Gorgeous decorative screens, splendid palaces, and severely simple teahouses were produced during this period. The decorative arts were especially brilliant, and the lacquers, colorful textiles, and rustic teawares are universally regarded as masterpieces. But it is perhaps in the domestic architecture of this period that the most influential and classical statement of Japanese art was made. The Edo period produced the *Ukiyo-e* prints which had such a great influence on the painters of the Impressionist and Postimpressionist movements, and these centuries saw the flourishing of traditional folk art, in which the popular and almost universal nature of Japanese artistic sensibility finds its most remarkable expression. By the late nineteenth century all these great traditions had exhausted themselves, and European influences began to transform the art of the Far East.

Chronological Table

	CHINA	KOREA	JAPAN
5000 B.C.			
3000 B.C.			Early Jomon 4500–3000 B.C.
			Middle Jomon 3000–2000 B.C.
2000 B.C.	Prehistoric Pottery Culture c. 2500–1500 B.C.		
1000 B.C.	Shang c. 1500–1000 B.C. Chou c. 1000–200 B.C.	Prehistoric Period	Late Jomon 2000–200 B.C.
Time of Christ	Han Empire c. 200 B.C.–A.D. 200	Three Kingdoms 57 B.C.–A.D. 668	Yayoi 200 B.C.–A.D. 200
A.D. 500	Six Dynasties c. A.D. 200–600	United Silla A.D. 668–935	Gravemound Period A.D. 200–550 Asuka A.D. 552–645
A.D. 1000	T'ang c. A.D. 600–900 Sung A.D. 960–1280	Koryo A.D. 918–1392	Nara A.D. 645–794 Heian A.D. 794–1185 Kamakura A.D. 1185–1333
	Yuan A.D. 1280–1368		Muromachi A.D. 1333–1573
		Yi Dynasty A.D. 1392–1910	
A.D. 1500	Ming A.D. 1368–1644		Momoyama A.D. 1573–1615
	Ch'ing A.D. 1644–1912		Edo A.D. 1615–1868
A.D. 1900	Modern A.D. 1912 to Present		Modern A.D. 1868 to Present

The oldest of the Neolithic civilizations of Eastern Asia is the Jomon civilization of prehistoric Japan. Among the works of art produced during this age the most interesting are the clay figures, believed to represent female fertility deities, which date from the second and first millenniums B. C. Like the Stone Age idols of prehistoric Europe, they emphasize the pubic region, the breasts, and the thighs, suggesting that these figures had some magical purpose. Another typical element of the clay images is the large eyes which give these idols a strange and mysterious quality.

Fertility idol. Clay, height 10⅜″. Late Jomon period, first millennium B.C. Museum of Fine Arts, Boston

Jar with molded design. Clay, height 12⅝″. Middle Jomon period, third millennium B.C. Welch Collection, Cambridge, Mass.

Jar with molded design. Clay, height c. 11³/₄″. Middle Jomon period, third millennium B. C. Kondo Collection, Niigata

The bulk of Jomon material consists of various types of clay vessels which were decorated with cord-impressed or molded designs. The best of these were made during the third millennium B. C., or the Middle Jomon period. The designs are often bizarre, with strange projecting and receding forms which show the remarkable sculptural feeling of the Jomon—certainly a more inventive and original people than any other Neolithic potters. The peculiar forms of their vessels were no doubt symbolical in nature, but it is not known what they were supposed to mean.

Jar with painted design. Clay, height 18″. Prehistoric
China, c. 2000 B. C. Chait Galleries, New York

The Neolithic pottery of China, which began later and flourished primarily from the middle of the third to the
middle of the second millennium, used very different shapes and decorative designs. Instead of weird sculptural
forms, the emphasis is on the simple beauty of the shapes, and these jars and bowls already reveal the uniquely

Jar with painted design. Clay, height 14$\frac{1}{8}$". Pre-historic China, c. 2000 B. C. Seattle Art Museum

Chinese gift for ceramic form. They are also outstanding for their painted decorations, which show the strong feeling for calligraphic line so typical of the later Chinese. The designs themselves consist of spirals, wavy lines, bands, squares, triangles, and an occasional styled figure, all of which were no doubt magical in purpose.

THE MAGIC BRONZE ART OF ANCIENT CHINA

The first historical civilization of the Far East was that of Shang China, which emerged around 1500 B. C. in the Yellow River valley of northern China, with its most important center in Anyang. The outstanding works

Tsun-shaped wine vessel. Bronze, height 11¹/₄″. Shang period, c. 1200 B. C. Morse Collection, New York

of art were bronze ceremonial vessels employed in the worship of the forces of nature and the spirits of ancestors. A large number have been found in tombs, and the best rank with the masterpieces of metalwork of all times. Used for offerings of wine and food to the spirits, they were given as presents on important official occasions and placed in the tombs of Shang aristocracy. These vessels, which the Chinese have always valued, are looked upon as the most important artistic production of ancient China.

Chia-shaped wine vessel. Bronze, height 33¹/₂″. Shang period, c. 1200 B. C. Morse Collection, New York

Various shapes were used for the bronze vessels, many of which were decorated with elaborate ornamental designs, often in the form of magic animals which symbolized the forces of nature. While some of these are derived from real animals, others, like the dragon, are completely imaginary, or else they are composite creatures of a fantastic kind. The central motif in many of these designs is the stylized tiger mask, called *t'ao t'ieh*, a symbol of the earth, and the dragon, which stood for clouds, rain, and sky. Many other animals—birds of all kinds, cicadas, snakes, bulls, elephants, water buffaloes—also occur, while human figures are only rarely represented.

Ting-shaped food vessel. Bronze, height
8″. Shang period, c. 1300 B. C. Morse
Collection, New York

Hu-shaped wine vessel. Bronze, height 24³/₄″. Middle Chou period, c. 800 B. C. Morse Collection, New York

After some five hundred years, the Shang rulers were replaced by a new dynasty called Chou. The earliest productions of the Chou metalworkers are hardly distinguishable from those of the Shang, but by the middle of the ninth century B. C., the Middle Chou period, and even more during the Late Chou, a completely new

Hu-shaped wine vessel. Bronze, height 13″. Late Chou period, c. 500 B. C. Morse Collection, New York

style emerged. The magic symbols of the Shang people first disintegrated and finally disappeared, and more formal, abstract designs took their place. The shapes of the bronzes also changed, with many of the older types no longer being used, and rounded shapes with designs in concentric bands becoming more common.

Among the new shapes which were evolved during the Late Chou period (600–200 B. C.) is the winepot with a spout, which is the ancestor of the teapot used all over the world today. The Chou metalworkers also developed new techniques, such as elaborate inlays of gold, silver, and turquoise. The ornamentation tended to be more abstract than those of the Shang, and no longer projected beyond the surface of the vessel. Although both the shapes and decorative designs lack some of the expressive power of the best of the Shang bronzes, they often have an elegance and sophistication which reflect the more advanced civilization.

Ho-shaped winepot. Bronze, height 8¹/₂″. Late Chou period, c. 500 B. C. Museum of Fine Arts, Boston (Bernat Collection, on loan)

Tui-shaped food vessel. Bronze with turquoise inlay, height 15⁷/₈″. Late Chou period, c. 400 B. C. Fogg Art Museum, Cambridge, Mass.

Dish with painted designs. Lacquer on wood, diameter 12¹/₄″. Late
Chou period, c. 300 B. C. Freer Gallery of Art, Washington, D. C.

Carved pendant with bird-and-dragon design. Jade, height 2¹/₈″. Late Chou period,
c. 400 B. C. William Rockhill Nelson Gallery and Mary Atkins Museum, Kansas City

In addition to bronze, many other mediums were used by the craftsmen of ancient China. The most important was jade, which the Chinese from the earliest times had regarded as both auspicious and beautiful. Sacred emblems as well as ornaments were fashioned from jade, often showing not only technical skill but great beauty of design. The other important medium was lacquer, which was usually applied to a wooden base. The surviving lacquer vessels are particularly interesting for their graceful painted decorations, which may give us some idea of the paintings of the period.

During the Late Chou period, sculpture began to emerge as a major art form. Although usually small in scale, the best of the Chou carvings are truly sculptural, with a fine feeling for plastic form. Both animal and human figures are represented, usually in a rather naturalistic manner. Among the mediums used were wood, often lacquered or painted, jade, bronze, and clay. Perhaps the most significant development of Late Chou sculpture was the emergence of the human figure as a major subject, reflecting the humanistic tendencies of the age.

Torso of horse. Painted wood, height 9″. Late Chou period, c. 300 B. C. Singer Collection, Summit, New Jersey

Birds and snakes. Lacquered wood, height 53³/₄″. Late ▶ Chou period, c. 400 B. C. Cleveland Museum of Art

THE ART OF THE HAN EMPIRE AND GRAVEMOUND JAPAN

With the beginning of the Han period around 200 B. C., Chinese art entered a new phase, in which painting, monumental architecture, and large-scale sculpture began to replace the ritual vessels as the most important forms of artistic expression. Unfortunately little of the major art has survived, but the fragments of wall paintings and the pictorial designs engraved on stone slabs or impressed on clay tiles suggest the sophistication and beauty of the lost art. The emphasis is upon line, which is treated in the animated and inspired way so characteristic of the Chinese tradition.

◄ Painted tomb tile. Pigment on clay, height 7³/₄″. Han period c. A. D. 200. Museum of Fine Arts, Boston

Impressed tile. Clay, height 49″. Han period, c. 200 B. C. Caro Collection, New York

Horse's head. Jade, length 7¹/₈". Han period, c. A. D. 100. Fogg Art Museum, Cambridge, Mass.

Dragon. Gilded bronze, length 4³/₄″. Han period, c. A. D. 200. Fogg Art Museum, Cambridge, Mass.

Han sculpture shows this same feeling for linear movement and dynamic energy, qualities which are evident in the wonderful representation of dragons and other mythological beasts. Particularly fine are the numerous figures of horses, which the Han sculptors rendered with spirit and skill. While some of these sculptures were executed in stone on a large scale, others were smaller in size and made of metal, wood, clay, or jade—materials which Chinese carvers had used since ancient times. In all these works the emphasis is on the underlying sculptural form rather than on detail or a naturalistic likeness.

Among the most interesting works are the numerous clay vessels and figures found in the Han tombs. Often thousands of objects of all types were discovered in a single imperial grave. They represent not only the people of the time but houses, watchtowers, animals, and various utensils, which, taken together, give a vivid sense of the material culture of the time. Although produced from molds in huge quantities, their purpose being to accompany the spirits of the dead to the world beyond, these objects are often very beautiful in form and design. The same is also true of the clay vessels, some of which are masterpieces of pottery.

Watchtower for tomb. Clay, height 37″. Han period, c. A. D. 200. Fogg Art Museum, Cambridge, Mass.

Hu-shaped jar. Glazed clay, height 14¹/₄″. Han period, c. 100 B.C. Fogg Art Museum, Cambridge, Mass.

39

Belt buckle. Gold and jade, length 8⁵/₈″. Han period,
c. 200 B. C. Fogg Art Museum, Cambridge, Mass.

Belt hook with deer design. Jade, length 2³/₄″. Han period, ▶
c. 200 B. C. Fogg Art Museum, Cambridge, Mass.

The Han period, during which China was united and prosperous, was an age of material splendor. This is
evident in the decorative arts, which flourished as never before. Beautiful metalwork, such as mirrors, belt
buckles, and ornaments, as well as jade carvings, lacquers, and textiles of superb craftsmanship, were produced for the ruling classes. These works, although usually small in scale and utilitarian in function, were
executed with great care and show the remarkable feeling for design which is characteristic of Chinese decorative arts throughout the ages.

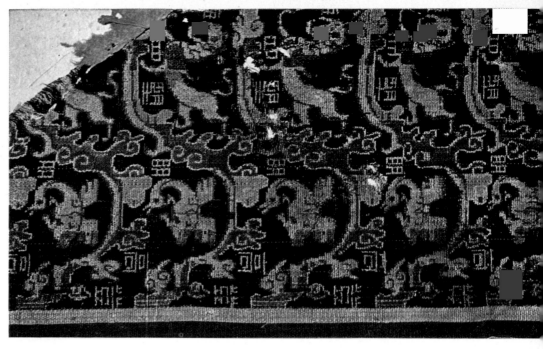

Fragment of textile with flying ducks and tigers, from East Turkestan. Silk, length c. 12½″. Han period, 100 B.C.–A.D. 200. Central Asian Antiquities Museum, New Delhi

Ordos-type plaque in form of a mule. Silver, length 5³/₄″.
Han period, 206 B.C. – A.D. 220. British Museum, London

Two Ordos-type hunting knives. Bronze, length of upper 7″; length of lower
8″. Late Chou period, seventh–sixth century B.C. British Museum, London

Ornamental plaque with animal design. Gold inlaid with blue glass, length 3¹/₂″.
Scythian style from Iran, c. seventh century B.C. University Museum, Philadelphia

Since China under the Han rulers expanded westward into Central Asia, it came into close contact with the people of the steppes, who had evolved an artistic tradition of their own that influenced Han decorative art. A nomadic people who roamed about the vast regions of Central Asia and Siberia, their art consisted largely of small metal objects ornamented with animal forms which were connected with hunting magic. The most splendid of these works are the golden cups and golden ornaments which were found in the tombs of Scythian rulers at archaeological sites in Russia, and which today are largely in Russian museums.

Ordos plaque. Bronze, length 5⁷/₈″. Han period, c. 100 B.C. William
Rockhill Nelson Gallery and Mary Atkins Museum, Kansas City

The influence of the art of the nomads is most apparent in the metal objects found in the Ordos region, where this culture and that of China met. Here swords and daggers made of bronze have been discovered in large quantities, along with plaques decorated with animals derived from ancient Siberian and Persian art. Horses and reindeer are prominent, as well as the familiar Persian motif of a tiger or lion attacking a bull or some other horned animal. Highly stylized and always small in scale, these sculptures render animals in a vital and expressive way.

Jar. Clay, height 16¹/₈″. Yayoi period,
c. A. D. 200. Kurashiki Museum of
Archaeology

In Japan the Jomon culture had been succeeded by a more advanced civilization from the continent, which is called Yayoi after the district of Tokyo where remains of this culture were first found. While the Jomon people had made hand-formed pottery with molded and impressed designs, the Yayoi used the potter's wheel and produced work whose beauty lies in the shape of the vessel rather than in its surface decoration. In this way, Yayoi art anticipates the peculiar sensibility found in the work of later periods, unlike the art of the Jomon, which was produced by a Caucasoid people not related to the modern Japanese, but to the Ainus.

Tazza-shaped dish. Clay, height 7¹/₂″. Yayoi period, c. A. D. 200. Munsterberg Collection, New Paltz, New York

The most striking works of prehistoric Japan were the cylindrical grave figures, or *haniwa*, which were set in a circle around the foot and top of the huge mounds built over the tombs of the dead rulers. Very abstract in form and naïve in expression, they appeal to modern taste and are generally regarded as the finest of the primitive sculptures of Eastern Asia. Like the Han grave figures, they are also interesting as a reflection of contemporary culture.

Haniwa horse. Clay, height 8″. Gravemound period, c. A. D. 500. Fogg Art Museum, Cambridge, Mass.

Haniwa figure. Clay, height 26³/₈″. Gravemound period, c. A. D. 500. Museum of Fine Arts, Boston

Of the art forms evolved during this early phase, the one which had the most vital influence on the culture of later periods was the Shinto shrine. Although the present-day structures are not the original buildings, they follow the ancient models very closely and no doubt reflect the kind of sacred buildings found in Japan

Izumo shrine. Wood and thatch. Traditional style, present structure built 1744. Izumo, Shimane Prefecture

during these early centuries. Constructed on stilts and using unpainted wood, with heavy, overhanging thatch roofs, they resemble the chieftain's hut of Indo-China and Polynesia, suggesting the Southern affinity of the Japanese people.

Miniature Shinto shrines. Wood and cypress bark. Kamakura period, thirteenth century. Enjoji, Nara Prefecture

Bodhisattva Kuan Yin. Gilded bronze, height 13¹⁄₈″.
Six Dynasties period, fourth century A. D. Fujii Museum, Kyoto

Seated Buddha. Gilded bronze, height 11¹/₂″. Six Dynasties period, fourth century A.D. Fogg Art Museum, Cambridge, Mass.

The collapse of the Han dynasty during the second century of the Christian era was followed by years of chaos and disunity which are known as the Six Dynasties period. It was at this time that Buddhism and Buddhist art were introduced from India. The earliest of the Buddhist images were based on Greco-Buddhist or Central Asian prototypes, and were often made by foreign monks who had come to China as missionaries. The two most common iconographical types were the image of the seated Buddha Sakyamuni and that of the standing Bodhisattva of Mercy and Compassion, called Kuan Yin in China.

53

Flying Apsaras from T'ien Lung-shan. ▶
Stone, height 30". Six Dynasties period,
sixth century A. D. Fogg Art Museum,
Cambridge, Mass.

Bodhisattva Maitreya. Stone, height
72". Six Dynasties period, c. A. D.
500. Museum of Fine Arts, Boston

Although bronze, wood, lacquer, and clay were used by the Chinese Buddhist sculptors, the bulk of the surviving images are made of stone. Many of them come from the great cave sites at Yün-kang and Lung-mên. Here pious monks and humble craftsmen carved thousands of Buddhist icons out of the living rock. The finest of them, made under the Northern Wei dynasty during the later fifth and early sixth centuries, are moving works of religious sculpture in which the otherworldly feeling of Buddhism is expressed in an abstract, linear style resembling that of Romanesque Europe.

During the second half of the sixth century, renewed Indian influences made the style of the sculptures somewhat softer and more sensuous, resulting in works of a gentle beauty. The Buddhist ideal of serenity achieved by overcoming desire is movingly portrayed in these works, which rank among the great religious sculptures of all times. The faces of the Buddhas and bodhisattvas, with a beatific smile hovering over the lips, are especially beautiful and give profound expression to the religious ideal of Buddhism.

Head of a bodhisattva from Lung-mên. Stone, height 16″. Six Dynasties period, early sixth century A. D. Morse Collection, New York

Head of a bodhisattva. Stone, height 9¹/₄″. Six Dynasties period, later sixth century A. D. Fogg Art Museum, Cambridge, Mass.

Sakyamuni and the Buddha of the Past. Gilded bronze, height 4½". Six Dynasties period, sixth century A. D. Freer Gallery of Art, Washington, D. C.

In addition to the Buddha Sakyamuni, the founder of the religion, a multitude of other Buddhas and sacred beings are represented in Chinese sculpture. Among those who are often seen are Maitreya, the Buddha of the Future, and Prabhutaratna, the Buddha of the Past, who is usually portrayed seated side by side with Sakyamuni. In the altarpieces, the Buddha is often shown flanked by two bodhisattvas, or Buddhist saints, and surrounded by monks, angels, and guardian figures.

Buddhist altar. Gilded bronze, height 8¾". Sui period, ▶
dated A. D. 599. Sickman Collection, Kansas City

Buddha receiving a follower. Fresco painting. Six Dynasties peri- ▶
od, sixth century A. D. Thousand Buddha Caves at Tun-huang

Jataka scene showing Buddha's previous incarnation as a deer. Fresco painting.
Six Dynasties period, sixth century A. D. Thousand Buddha Caves at Tun-huang

Buddhist painting was of major importance during the Six Dynasties period, but very little has survived. The frescoes in the Caves of the Thousand Buddhas at Tun-huang, the westernmost outpost of Chinese civilization, no doubt reflect the Sixth Dynasty style with their complex iconography and flat, abstract manner. Although the works are by provincial painters, most of whom were probably monks, these frescoes are of great artistic beauty with vivid colors and tense linear forms. The subjects are usually taken either from Buddhist legends relating to the previous incarnations of the Buddha, the so-called Jataka stories, or from Buddhist scriptures. However, the great historical interest of these pictures lies not only in their Buddhist subjects but also in their manner of depicting the landscape and the human figure, which reflects the artistic style current at that time.

Standing bodhisattva. Stone, height 66¹/₈″. Sui period, c. A.D. 600. Fogg Art Museum, Cambridge, Mass.

In A. D. 589, after three centuries of disunity, China was united under the Sui dynasty. Although this house lasted for only thirty years, the artistic output was immense, for the Sui rulers were great patrons of Buddhism and Buddhist art. In fact some of the loveliest Chinese Buddhist sculptures date from this time. Their style, which emphasizes the cylindrical shape of the figure, is derived from Gupta India and has a marked feeling for the plastic form.

Standing bodhisattva. Stone, height 52″. Sui period, c. A. D. 600. William Rockhill Nelson Gallery and Mary Atkins Museum, Kansas City

Torso of a bodhisattva from T'ien Lung-shan. Stone, height 26¼". T'ang period, c. A. D. 650. William Rockhill Nelson Gallery and Mary Atkins Museum, Kansas City

Head of a Buddha. Stone, height 12½". T'ang period, c. A. D. 650. Morse Collection, New York

With the advent of the T'ang dynasty during the early seventh century, a new style of Buddhist art emerged, which was characterized by a fuller and more naturalistic manner. Here again the bulk of the surviving images come from the great cave sites of northern China, notably Lung-mên and T'ien Lung-shan. The soft forms and sensuous beauty of the sculptures indicate a strong Indian influence in contrast to the most abstract, linear manner indigenous to China.

Guardian figure. Lacquer, height
22⁷/₈″. T'ang period, c. A. D. 700.
Museum of Fine Arts, Boston

Seated Buddha. Gilded bronze, height 6½″. T'ang period, c. A. D. 650. Private collection, Japan

In addition to the Buddhist figures carved into the walls of the caves, there were freestanding sculptures made from stone, bronze (which was usually gilded), lacquer, wood, or clay. An innovation of the T'ang period was the making of hollow lacquer images which were very light and thus could be carried in religious processions. Taken as a whole, it is during the T'ang period, which lasted from the seventh to the ninth century, that Chinese sculpture celebrated its greatest triumphs.

Mountain landscape showing Hsüan Tsang returning from India. Fresco painting. T'ang period, seventh century A. D. Thousand Buddha Caves at Tun-huang

Landscape with rising sun and Queen Vaidehi. Fresco painting. T'ang ▶ period, seventh century A. D. Thousand Buddha Caves at Tun-huang

The numerous T'ang period wall paintings, such as the ones in the great cave temples at Tun-huang, not only represent all kinds of Buddhist subjects, notably paradise scenes showing the celestial realm of the Buddha Amitabha, but also portray landscapes which are of particular interest in reflecting the early phases of Chinese landscape painting, of which very little has survived. Although they were intended merely as a background for scenes from Buddhist legend, these paintings show the typically Chinese landscape with its suggestive rendering of space and atmosphere.

Court ladies playing music. Ink and color on silk, height 16¹/₂″. Style of Late T'ang period, tenth century A. D. Art Institute of Chicago

In addition to the Buddhist work, there was a flourishing secular art during the T'ang period. Literary records tell of landscape and figure paintings which were praised for the vigor of their brushwork and the loftiness of their conception. Executed on paper or silk, or on the walls of buildings which have long since vanished, few have survived, and most of the extant works are probably later copies of T'ang originals. Particularly fine are the figure paintings showing scenes from contemporary life and portraying statesmen and court ladies.

71

Dragon head. Glazed clay, height 15³/₄″. Sung period, eleventh century. Stöcker Collection, St. Astier, France

Winged chimera. Stone, height 42¹/₂″. Six Dynasties period, sixth ▶
century A. D. Albright-Knox Art Gallery, Buffalo, New York

Secular sculpture flourished during both the Six Dynasties and T'ang periods. Among the most impressive of the stone statues are the giant chimeras which guard the tombs of the Chinese emperors at Nanking and whose dynamic and powerful forms show the native Chinese tradition at its very best. Equally impressive are the bronze images of various beasts, proof that in this medium Chinese artists continued to produce outstanding and expressive works of art.

Horse for a tomb. Painted clay, height 14¹/₄″. T'ang period,
seventh century A. D. Fogg Art Museum, Cambridge, Mass.

During the T'ang period, the animal most frequently represented was the horse. Most famous, perhaps, are
the large-scale relief carvings in stone which decorated the tomb of the T'ang Emperor T'ai Tsung; but most
remarkable are the innumerable clay figures of horses which have been found in the tombs. Although the
Chinese themselves did not consider them to be works of art, these small-scale sculptures are among the finest

representations of horses ever produced. No other people portrayed this animal so frequently in its art, not only in stone and clay, but also in wood, bronze, jade, ivory, and precious metals. Some of these works are monumental sculptures like the famous equestrian monument of the Han cavalry general Ho Ch'ü-ping; others are exquisite little carvings such as the lovely jade horse's head carved in Han times (p. 36).

Relief carving of horse and groom. Stone, height 68″. T'ang period, seventh century A. D. University Museum, Philadelphia

Other T'ang grave figures represent the court ladies of the period. They are not only charming figurines but interesting in showing the fashions of the day, the ideals of feminine beauty, and the life led by the T'ang ladies. Although many of these figures were executed in unadorned clay, others were glazed with bright colors. Among the most delightful are the dancers and musicians, which show the entertainments performed at the T'ang court and which were placed in the tombs so that the spirits of the dead might enjoy these pleasures in the other world. Although mass-produced in huge quantities and thought of, not as works of art, but merely as tomb furniture, these small terra cottas have very real artistic merit and today rightly enjoy great popularity among collectors. In fact, they are so much in demand that large numbers of fakes are produced, so that the bulk of such figures on the art market are not from the T'ang period but are modern forgeries.

◄ Group of female musicians. Painted clay, height 6¹/₄". T'ang period, seventh century A.D. Museum of Decorative Arts, Frankfurt

Court lady for a tomb. Glazed clay, height 10¹/₄". T'ang period, seventh century A.D. Munsterberg Collection. New Paltz, New York

Jar. Glazed clay, height 6$^1/_4$". T'ang period, seventh century A. D. Munsterberg Collection, New Paltz, New York

Amphora. Glazed clay, height 20$^3/_4$". T'ang period, ▶ seventh century A. D. Museum of Fine Arts, Boston

Also outstanding were the ceramic vessels of the T'ang period, which some critics consider the finest pottery ever made in China. Certainly the strong, simple shapes and the subdued colors of the glazes, especially the deep greens and creamy white, are very remarkable. Foreign influences from Persia and the Byzantine West are apparent in some of the shapes and designs, for T'ang China was a cosmopolitan culture, and people from all over the world could be found in the capital at Ch'ang-an.

Mirror with animal design. Bronze, diameter 6¹/₂″. Sui period, c. A. D. 600. William Rockhill Nelson Gallery and Mary Atkins Museum, Kansas City

All the other crafts flourished during this period, reflecting the rich material culture of the time. The mirrors, often inlaid with patterns in gold and silver, were particularly fine, and so were the woven and embroidered

Mirror with bird-and-flower design. Bronze with gold and silver inlay, diameter 8¹/₄″. T'ang period, seventh century A.D. Museum of Fine Arts, Boston

fabrics, in which the beauty of the designs was worked out with great technical skill. No age of Chinese art ever experienced such a florescence of all the decorative arts as did that of the T'ang rulers.

Departure of Siddharta. Fresco painting from Koço, Chinese Turkestan, height 10³/₄″. T'ang period, ninth century A. D. Museum of Indian Art, Berlin

Bordering upon western China were the great expanses of Central Asia, where Buddhist communities had flourished for many centuries. During the Six Dynasties period their art had largely reflected Indian influences, but now, with the expansion of Chinese power into Central Asia, Chinese influences became predomi-

Teaching Buddha. Fresco painting from Bezeklik, Chinese Turkestan, height 17³/₄″. T'ang period, ninth century A.D. Museum of Indian Art, Berlin

nant. This is most evident in the magnificent wall paintings uncovered beneath the sands at the monasteries of Chinese Turkestan. Here scenes from Buddhist legend are rendered in a style obviously derived from Chinese prototypes.

Uigur prince. Fresco painting from Koço, height 23⅝". T'ang period, ninth century A. D. Museum of Indian Art, Berlin

Nestorian worshiper. Fresco painting from Koço, height 17⅛". T'ang period, ninth century A. D. Museum of Indian Art, Berlin

Particularly interesting in these frescoes are the numerous portraits of donors, for they represent people of a great variety of racial and cultural backgrounds: not only Central Asians and Chinese, but also Indians, Sassanian Persians, Tartars, Turks, Nestorian Christians, and Uigurs. Although Chinese influences dominated much of this art during the T'ang period, other traditions were also reflected in the painting of Central Asia, notably those of late classical art, of Persia, and of India.

Textile with dragon design. Silk embroidery from Koço, height 4¹/₂".
T'ang period, ninth century A.D. Museum of Indian Art, Berlin

Bodhisattva. Silk-embroidered cotton, height 15". T'ang ▶
period, ninth century A.D. Museum of Indian Art, Berlin

Next to the wall paintings, the most remarkable finds at these Buddhist sanctuaries were the textile fragments, which had been beautifully preserved in the dry desert climate. In fact, many of the finest Chinese textiles of this date were found in Central Asia, indicating how popular Chinese fabrics were even beyond the borders of their empire. Many of the decorative motifs were Buddhist, while others reflect the native Chinese culture, as in the designs of dragons.

KOREAN AND JAPANESE ART UNDER BUDDHIST INSPIRATION

From China, Buddhism spread to Korea. Although derived from Chinese sources, Korean Buddhist art developed qualities which give it its own character. Outstanding among the early Buddhist monuments of Korea are the stone pagodas, which combine strength with beautiful proportions, and the deeply moving images of Maitreya, the Buddha of the Future, seated in divine meditation, which are among the most profound and beautiful of all the Buddhist images of the Far East. The Buddhist art of China and Japan is much better known than that of Korea, which, as a relatively small country located between two giants, has always suffered neglect in this and many other areas; but Korean Buddhist art is actually very remarkable. Indeed, it was these Korean monuments which first inspired the Buddhist art of Japan.

◀ Pagoda of Punhwang-sa. Stone and brick. Old Silla period, seventh century A. D. Kyongju, Korea

Maitreya in meditation. Bronze, height 8¹/₄″. Old Silla period, seventh century A. D. Fogg Art Museum, Cambridge, Mass.

During the sixth and seventh centuries, the Buddhist art of Korea was influenced by that of the Six Dynasties and Sui China; but in the eighth century, after the Silla dynasty had united Korea, the art came under the influence of the T'ang. The bronze and stone sculptures of this period are particularly fine, reflecting the full-bodied T'ang style and yet showing certain modifications in the handling of the forms which clearly distinguish them from their Chinese prototypes.

Rubbing of Apsaras from temple bell. Bronze, height 59″. United Silla period, eighth century A. D. Kyongju Museum, Korea

Standing Buddha. Gilded bronze, height 5¹/₂″. United Silla period, seventh century A. D. Fogg Art Museum, Cambridge, Mass.

Gate at Horyuji. Wood and tile.
Asuka period, seventh century A. D.
Nara

The earliest Japanese Buddhist art was based on Korean models, for Buddhism had been brought to Japan by missionaries from Korea. This first phase is called the Asuka period, after the district in which the capital was located. The finest Asuka works are found in Nara, especially at Horyuji, which was one of the great religious centers of the time. Among the buildings at Horyuji today are some of the oldest wooden structures in the world; and the Kondo, or Golden Hall, contains some of the best of the early Japanese Buddhist sculptures and paintings.

Pagoda of Hokkiji. Wood and
tile. Early Nara period, seventh
century A. D. Nara

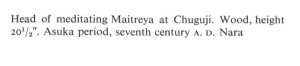

Head of meditating Maitreya at Chuguji. Wood, height 20¹/₂″. Asuka period, seventh century A. D. Nara

Among the images at the Horyuji monastery and the neighboring Chuguji convent are some of the greatest icons in all Buddhist art. Carved in wood or cast in bronze, they are works of extraordinary beauty and depth of feeling. Although profoundly influenced by Korean models, they show the Japanese genius for sculpture which had already been expressed in the *haniwa* grave figures of prehistoric times. Particularly beautiful are the images in wood, a medium which the Japanese carvers have always found the most congenial, while they hardly ever worked in stone. The two most celebrated examples of such early wooden images are the representation of the standing Kannon Bosatsu, the Japanese form of the Chinese Kuan Yin or the Indian Avalokitesvara, the Bodhisattva of Mercy and Compassion, and the seated image of the Buddha of the Future, Maitreya, who is known as Miroku in Japanese.

Standing Kannon. Painted wood and metal, height 80$^1/_4$″.
Asuka period, seventh century A. D. Nara

Tamamushi shrine at Horyuji. Lacquer on wood, height 91³/₈″. Asuka period, seventh century A. D. Nara

Very little Asuka painting has survived. The most important example is the Tamamushi shrine, which is also located at Horyuji. On its sides are a series of paintings, called the Jataka scenes, which represent the Buddha in his previous incarnations. The style is very curvilinear and abstract, probably reflecting the painting which was being produced by the Koreans of that time. Some Japanese scholars have suggested that, if this is so, it would make these the earliest oil paintings in existence.

During the Nara period contact was established with T'ang China and, as a result, Japanese art came to be influenced by that of China rather than Korea. Numerous temples from this period are still extant, especially in the city of Nara, which at that time was the political and religious center of Japan. Since virtually no Chinese temples of this period have been preserved, these buildings are invaluable, not only for the history of Japanese architecture, but also for that of China.

Hokkedo at Todaiji. Wood and tile. Nara period, eighth century A. D. Nara

Yumedono at Horyuji. Wood and tile. Nara period, eighth century A. D. Nara

The basic mode of construction continued to be the post-and-lintel system which had been used by the earlier builders, but the Nara period structures, which reflected those of T'ang China, were far more complex in their construction and sophisticated in their design. Particularly fine are their beautiful proportions and the severe geometry of their forms, which have a great appeal for the modern artistic taste.

Eleven-headed Kannon at Shorinji. Dry lacquer, height 82¹/₄″. Nara period, eighth century A. D. Nara

Most critics regard the Buddhist sculpture of the Nara period as the high point in the development of Japanese sculpture. There are magnificent images of Buddhas, bodhisattvas, guardians, and monks. While the earlier statues were usually made of wood or bronze, the Nara sculptors also employed hollow lacquer and clay. This last medium was particularly favored for the guardian figures protecting the entrances to the temples.

Guardian figure at Horyuji. Clay and wood, height 10′ 10″. Nara period, eighth century A. D. Nara

Tile with bird design. Clay, height 11⁷/₈″. Nara period, eighth century A. D. Seattle Art Museum

While the most important icons were usually sculptures in the round, there are many Nara works which are executed in relief. Outstanding among these are the decorative metal panels, which show a wonderful sense of animated linear design, and the clay tiles, which, although made by ordinary craftsmen to decorate the roofs of the temples, are often of very real beauty.

Music-making Apsaras from Suien of the Yakushiji Pagoda. Bronze. Nara period, eighth century A. D. Nara

Amida paradise scene before the fire. Fresco, height ▶
10′ 3″. Nara period, eighth century A. D. Nara

Interior view of Kondo at Horyuji after the fire. Wood and
pigment on plaster. Nara period, eighth century A. D. Nara

The most important surviving examples of Buddhist painting from the Nara period were the frescoes decorating the walls of the Kondo, or Golden Hall, at Horyuji. Unfortunately, these unique treasures of ancient Buddhist art were largely destroyed by fire in 1949. However, the photographs and reproductions made before the fire give us a good idea of what they looked like. The four Buddhist paradises were represented, along with individual figures of bodhisattvas, and the style was typical of T'ang painting.

Eleven-headed Kannon from Horyuji
before the fire. Fresco, height 98⅜".
Nara period, eighth century A. D. Nara

Eleven-headed Kannon after the fire. Fresco, height 98³/₈″. Nara period, eighth century A.D. Nara

Although most of the frescoes were damaged beyond recognition, in some of the paintings the intense heat merely changed the chemical composition of the pigments, resulting in new and sometimes very lovely effects. It is interesting to compare photographs of the same picture taken before and after the fire. One of the most striking contrasts occurs in the Eleven-headed Kannon, for the painting had been covered by a funguslike black smut, which was removed by the fire, letting the image emerge more clearly.

THE EMERGENCE OF AN INDIGENOUS ART IN JAPAN

Japanese art of the Asuka and Nara periods had been greatly influenced by the art of the Asian continent. With the Late Heian period, especially during the tenth to twelfth centuries, the art developed a more indigenous character. This native tendency is most clearly apparent in the paintings of the *Yamato-e*, or Japanese school, which took its subjects from Japanese literature and history and represented a typically Japanese landscape with green, round-topped mountain scenery. The most famous of the Heian *Yamato-e* scrolls is that illustrating *The Tale of Genji*, the great literary classic of the eleventh century. Its emphasis upon narrative and its abstract, decorative feeling are very characteristic of the native Japanese tradition.

Scene from the *Tale of Genji*. Color on paper, height 8⁵/₈″. Heian period, twelfth century. Tokugawa Museum, Nagoya

Yamato-e-style landscape screen. Color on silk, height 39¹/₂″. ▶ Kamakura period, thirteenth century. Jingoji, Kyoto

同寅剋ニ信西う婦小路
志く火を放川これ四年ハ参仕禁制なと
西洞院乃岩所被捕
あまて天下静謐ありつ人ミまさに天る龍せ
朱き禁中も宮中兵四く太こ
ちうくなるまねク人ふつこ貴賤つかう三あつ

Section of *Heiji Monogatari* scroll. Color on paper, height 16³/₄″.
Kamakura period, thirteenth century. Museum of Fine Arts, Boston

While *Yamato-e* is a creation of the Heian period, the bulk of the surviving scrolls of this school date from the Kamakura period. A warlike age, the subjects were often scenes of military exploits rendered in a more detailed and realistic style than that of the earlier narrative scrolls. Perhaps the most outstanding of these works is the dramatic *Heiji Monogatari*, or Story of the Heiji Wars, consisting of three rolls, one of which is now in the Boston Museum.

Section of the *Honen Shonin* scroll showing birth of Honen. Ink and color on paper, height 16^1/$_2$". Kamakura period, thirteenth century. Seattle Art Museum

Other favorite subjects of the *Yamato-e* painters were the lives of celebrated monks and statesmen, and the legends associated with famous Buddhist temples and Shinto shrines. Usually a portion of text was followed by an illustration, with the beauty of both the calligraphy and painting forming an integral part of one artistic whole. One of the most popular of these scrolls recounts the tragic fate of the statesman Michizane, and another is about the life of Honen, one of the great religious teachers of the time. Each scroll might consist of several rolls containing numerous pictures, so that the full account of the story of the hero unfolds before the viewer in a continuing series. These narrative scrolls are not only interesting as works of art but often even more so as social documents depicting the life and customs of the time.

Section of *Kitano Tenjin Engi* scroll. Ink and color on paper, height 12$^1/_4$″. Kamakura period, thirteenth century. Seattle Art Museum

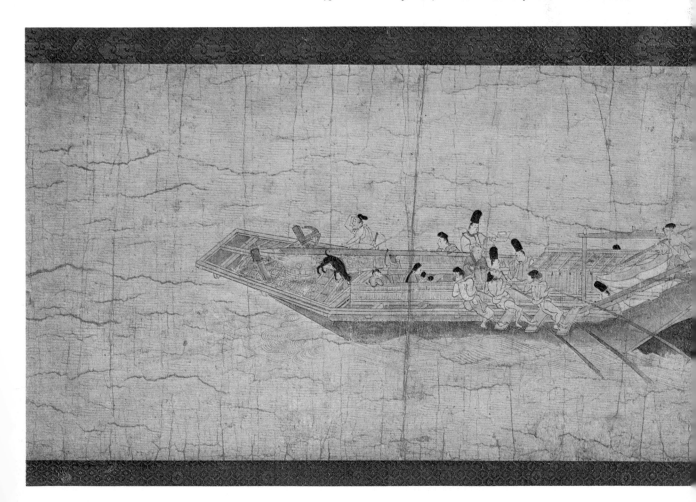

護摩諸尊種 略説有五類 廣説大瑜伽 陀毘盧遮那
如是一切事 隨明當應作 隨類作護摩 无上成就業
我今説護摩 由此速成就 由護摩業低 相應不間断
特進試鴻臚卿大興善寺三藏沙門大廣智不空奉 詔譯
金剛頂瑜伽護摩儀軌

Section of Buddhist scroll showing Paradise. Gold and silver on paper, height
$10^{1}/_{8}''$. Heian period, twelfth century. Fogg Art Museum, Cambridge, Mass.

Section of *Hell-fire* scroll. Color on paper, height $10^{1}/_{4}''$.
Kamakura period, thirteenth century. Seattle Art Museum

Other narrative scrolls dealt with Buddhist subjects, such as the joys of the souls who are reborn into the Western Paradise of the Buddha Amitabha, or the torments of hell-fire suffered by the damned as a punishment for their wicked deeds. Although ultimately based upon Chinese prototypes, these paintings represent an indigenous version of Buddhist art which reflects the native religious and artistic traditions that flourished during the Heian and Kamakura periods.

Besides the horizontal hand scrolls, Buddhist subjects were painted on vertical scrolls which were hung as icons on the walls of temples. They usually show Buddhist deities, such as Sakyamuni, the historical Buddha, or saints of the Buddhist pantheon like Kannon, the Bodhisattva of Mercy and Compassion, or Jizo, the patron saint of travelers and children. A uniquely Japanese type of Buddhist painting was the Raigo scroll in which the golden form of the Buddha Amitabha appears in the sky above green mountains.

Jizo Bosatsu. Color on silk, height 39³/₄″. Kamakura period, thirteenth century. Museum of Fine Arts, Boston

◄ Amida descending from the Western Paradise. Color on silk, height 47¹/₄″. Muromachi period, fourteenth century. Seattle Art Museum

While most of the hanging scrolls represented one deity, other works which were intended as important icons in major temples were considerably larger in size, with a complex composition involving dozens of figures, often grouped around a deity—usually either the Buddha Sakyamuni or the Buddha Amitabha in his Western Paradise. Among the paintings of Sakyamuni, the two most famous are the one representing the Death of the Buddha and the one showing Sakyamuni reappearing from his golden coffin to comfort his sorrowing mother.

Buddha's emergence from his golden coffin. Color on silk, height 62⁷/₈". Heian period, twelfth century. Chohoji, Kyoto

In addition to the paintings representing traditional Buddhist images, radically different
icons were created by the new esoteric sects
like the Shingon and the Tendai. The influence of mystic teachings from Hindu India
is reflected in those works, for the deities are
presented as strange, often grotesque, figures
rendered in a dramatic manner quite alien to
the graceful and harmonious forms used in
traditional Buddhist art. Among these new
deities, the most important are the Great
Kings, or *Myo-o*, of whom Fudo is the most
popular.

Fudo Myo-o. By Ryushu Myotaku. Ink and color on
silk, height 42 1/8". Muromachi period, fourteenth
century. Komor Collection, New York

Buddhist deity Muryo Rikiku. Colors on silk. Heian
period, ninth–tenth century. Hachiman-ko Monasteries, Wakayama Prefecture

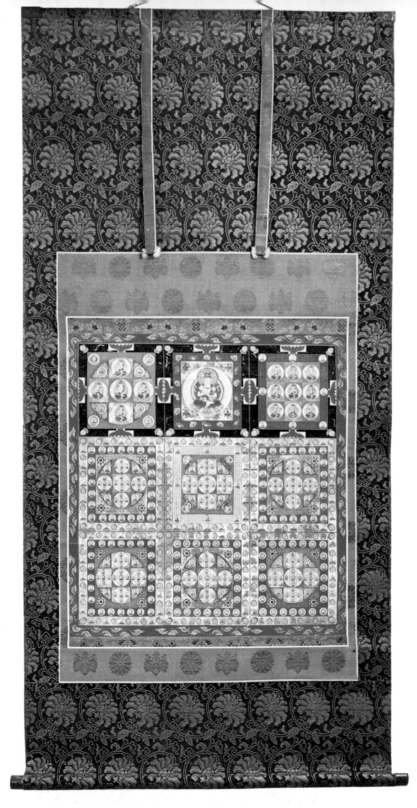

Other visual representations of these
new doctrines are the mandalas, or
magic diagrams, in which the Buddhist
conception of the world was rendered
in symbolical terms with the Great
Cosmic Buddha in the center, surrounded by a multitude of Buddhas and
sacred beings, who are supposed to be
a manifestation of the supreme Buddha.
A new religion combining Buddhism
and Shintoism also sprang up during
this period, and mandalas were painted,
in the center of which appeared Shinto
shrines as the focal point of the universe.

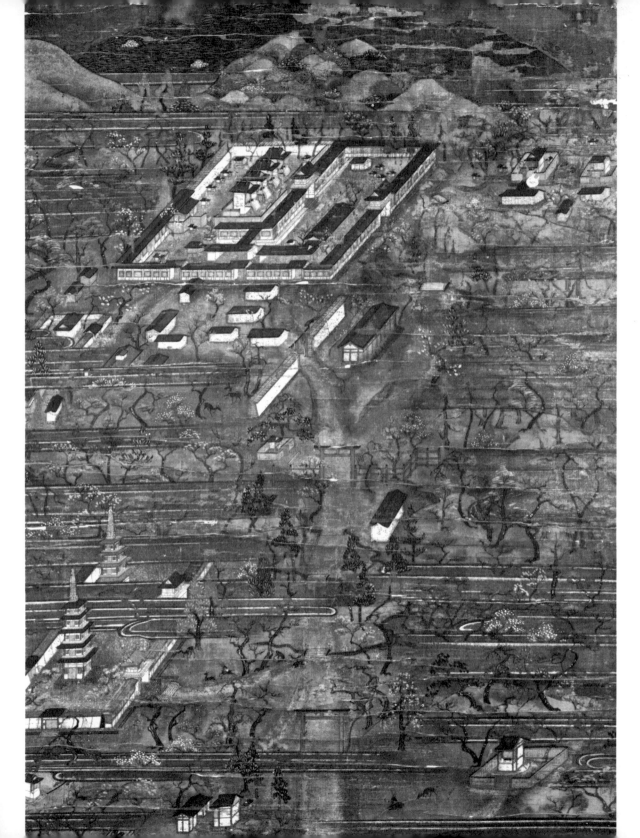

Flying Apsaras. Gilded wood, height 46″. Heian period, eleventh century. Seattle Art Museum

Kannon Bosatsu from Kofukuji. Gilded wood, height 16³/₄″. Heian period, ninth century A. D. Fogg Art Museum, Cambridge, Mass.

Although painting was no doubt the most important art of the Heian period, sculpture still played a significant role. The Heian carvings tended to be very graceful and elegant. The favorite medium was wood, which was usually gilded, so that the effect was quite splendid. As with painting, the tendency in sculpture was to create works in a more Japanese style, unlike the earlier periods which had slavishly copied continental models.

The Buddhas Amida and Yakushi. Wood, height c. 9' 10". Heian period, twelfth century. Ryuganji, Oita Prefecture

While the sculptures produced at the court in Kyoto reflected the refinement of the aristocratic society of the capital, the more provincial places turned out sculptures that are closer to the folk tradition. With their more

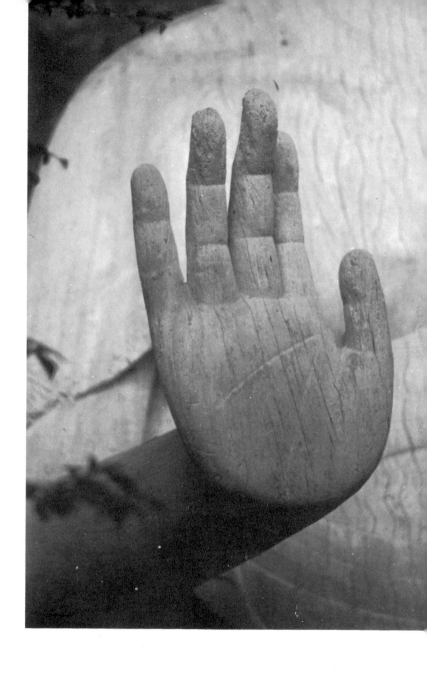

Hand of the Buddha Yakushi (detail of illustration on the facing page). Wood. Heian period, twelfth century. Ryuganji, Oita Prefecture

austere form and their emphasis upon the medium itself, these works appeal to the modern viewer who responds both to their simple strength and to their feeling for the material from which they are carved.

Guardian deity. Stone, height c. 9′
10″. Kamakura period, thirteenth
century. Fukoji, Oita Prefecture

Although the Japanese rarely used stone for freestanding sculptures, since the volcanic rock prevailing on the islands does not readily lend itself for carving, there are some outstanding examples of large-scale stone sculptures dating from the Heian period and located on the southern island of Kyushu. Like other provincial sculptures, they have certain affinities to folk carvings, with strong, simple shapes and a feeling of concentrated power.

Head of Dainichi Buddha. Stone, height of entire figure 8′ 10¹/₄″. Kamakura period, thirteenth century. Usuki, Oita Prefecture

In contrast to the elegance of the Heian images, the sculptures of the Kamakura period tend to be more realistic and more dramatic in expression. This is particularly evident in the numerous representations of guardian figures which were placed at the entrances of the Buddhist sanctuaries. Their contorted bodies and

fierce, scowling faces were meant to scare off any demons. The contrast between the expressive guardian figures and the serene images of the Buddhas shows the range of the Japanese sculptors, as well as the relationship of the style to the subject portrayed.

Guardian deity. Wood, height 63½".
Kamakura period, thirteenth century.
Kofukuji, Nara

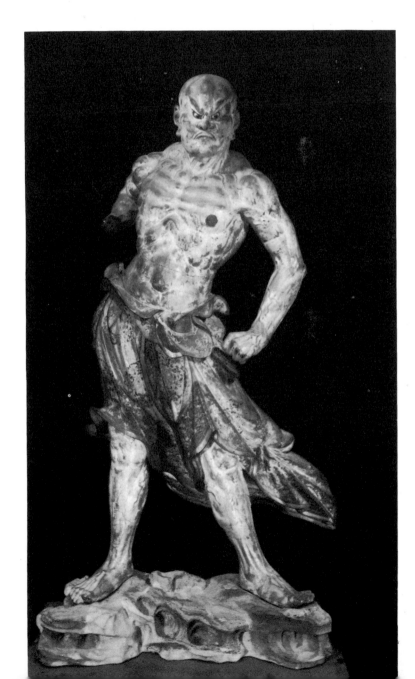

◀ Seated Buddha. Gilded lacquer, height 59".
Kamakura period, thirteenth century. Royal
Tropical Institute, Amsterdam

Head of Zen priest. Lacquer on wood, height 5¹/₂″. Muro-machi period, sixteenth century. Royal Tropical Institute, Amsterdam

Portrait of Shingon Abbot Eison. Wood, height 31¹/₂″. ▶
Kamakura period, fourteenth century. Museum of East Asian Art, Cologne

The realism so characteristic of the Kamakura period is most clearly seen in the statues of the abbots and teachers whose portraits were made in order to commemorate their earthly life. For this reason, it was important to show them in a lifelike manner so that later generations could revere their memory. Since they were monks rather than Buddhas or bodhisattvas, they were portrayed as real persons, showing their actual appearance and expression, which makes these works the first true portraits in Japanese art.

Kichijoten. Painted wood, height 40″. Kamakura period, thirteenth century. Alsdorf Collection, Winnetka, Illinois

The female figure, which was so important in the art of the West, was rarely represented in Japanese Buddhist art. One of the few exceptions is Kichijoten, the Japanese version of the Hindu goddess Sri Devi, who had found her way into the Buddhist pantheon as a goddess of Beauty and Good Fortune. She is usually represented as an elegant lady of the type which might have been found at the court in Kyoto.

Phœnix Hall of Byodoin. Wood and tiles. Heian period, eleventh century. Uji, Kyoto Prefecture

Among the architectural monuments of the Heian period, the most famous, as well as the most characteristic, is the Hōōdō, or Phoenix Hall, at Uji not far from Kyoto. Its graceful and elegant forms perfectly express the Heian spirit, while the more vigorous and powerful forms of the Great Gate at Todaiji in Nara embody the dominant feeling of the Kamakura period. Although the architectural style of both monuments derives ultimately from China, the design and construction have been modified to suit Japanese taste. The main

Main gate of Todaiji. Wood and tiles. Kamakura period, thirteenth century. Nara

building material in both periods continues to be wood, painted bright red, with gray tiles for the elaborate overhanging roofs and stone for the foundations. Although small in scale when compared to the great medieval cathedrals which were being built in Europe during the same centuries, they are, nevertheless, impressive and stately buildings which exactly mirror the spirit of medieval Japan.

Another celebrated example of Heian architecture is the pagoda of Daigoji, a temple also located at Uji. This work is a very beautiful example of Japanese wooden architecture with its graceful proportions and lovely silhouette. In contrast to the earlier pagodas, its construction is somewhat more complex, especially in its bracketing system, but otherwise it follows the traditional forms used by Japanese Buddhist builders throughout the ages.

Bracketing from the pagoda of Daigoji. Painted wood. Heian period, tenth century. Kyoto Prefecture

◀ Pagoda of Daigoji. Wood and tiles. Heian period, tenth century. Kyoto Prefecture

Cover of chest with floral designs and Apsarases and Buddhas. Gold and silver on lacquer, height 13³/₄". Heian period, tenth century. Formerly State Museums, Berlin

Inside lid of Urashima treasure box. Gold lacquer, length 11¹/₂″. Heian period, twelfth century. Seattle Art Museum

The Heian period, with its love of elegance and beauty, produced a wealth of decorative arts. The twelve-layer kimonos, in which each robe was made of a different colored silk, are vividly described in *The Tale of Genji*, but unfortunately none has been preserved. The most exquisite of the surviving Heian period crafts are the lacquer boxes which, with their lavish use of gold and silver decorations, reveal both beauty of design and excellence of craftsmanship.

THE REFINEMENT OF ART UNDER SUNG AND KORYO

With the Sung period Chinese painting, especially the landscapes, attained its most profound and artistically moving expression. Using only ink on silk or paper, the Sung artists caught the very essence of nature, or, as they said, the eternal Tao. The dominant theme is a recurring one, namely that of a tiny figure against picturesque trees, old rocks, and towering mountains in a misty atmosphere. Through these elements, the Sung painter strove to portray the majesty and mystery of the cosmos.

Sage Viewing the Moon. By Ma Yuan. Ink on silk, height 19⅝". Sung period, thirteenth century. Atami Museum

Bare Willows and Distant Mountains. By Ma Yuan. Ink on silk, height 9¹/₂″. Sung period, thirteenth century. Museum of Fine Arts, Boston

Mountains with Palaces in Snow.
By Fan K'uan. Ink on silk,
height 71⅝". Sung period, eleventh century. Museum of Fine
Arts, Boston

Sailboat in the Storm. By Hsia
Kuei. Ink on silk, diameter
9⅞". Sung period, thirteenth
century. Museum of Fine Arts,
Boston

In these paintings, man is depicted as a tiny part of the vastness of nature, often hardly visible at all. The onlooker is supposed to identify himself with these small figures, and thus feel through the painting the overwhelming grandeur of the cosmos, for in the Chinese view man was never thought of as the master of nature but rather as an insignificant part of the whole of creation.

In addition to hanging scrolls and album leaves, the Chinese also used horizontal hand scrolls in which the landscape was unrolled in front of the viewer as if he were traveling down a river valley in a boat. Here again, the emphasis is upon the grandeur of the mountains, the misty atmosphere, and the feeling of depth and space as the beautiful spectacle of the landscape unfolds. As the eleventh-century painter and critic Kuo Hsi said, these landscapes are truly wonderful.

River Landscape. Artist unknown. Ink on paper, height $16^7/_8''$. Sung period, twelfth century. Freer Gallery of Art, Washington, D. C.

Battling Demons in a Forest. By Li Sung. Ink on paper, height 8″. Sung
period, thirteenth century. Freer Gallery of Art, Washington, D. C.

Another major category, which had already been prominent during the T'ang period, was figure painting of all kinds. Not only were various types of men and women of Sung times portrayed, but Buddhist saints, Taoist sages, and all kinds of ghosts and demons were represented, with the latter forming the subject of some of the most inspired and fascinating of the Sung period figure paintings.

While most Sung paintings were monochromes, color, especially in figure paintings, was not uncommon; but the tones were always subtle, so that they were beautifully attuned to the silk on which they were painted. Nevertheless, even when the scrolls were colored, the main emphasis was still upon brushwork and linear design, which was such an essential aspect of the Chinese pictorial tradition which had had its beginnings in calligraphy.

Tribute Horse. Artist unknown. Ink and color on silk, height 32¹/₂″. Sung period, eleventh century. Metropolitan Museum of Art, New York

Detail of the painting on the facing page. Ink and color on silk. Sung period, eleventh century. Museum of Fine Arts, Boston

Portraiture in a Western sense does not really exist in Chinese art, for even when real persons were represented —officials, scholars, court ladies—the artist portrayed a generalized type rather than the naturalistic likeness of a specific person. Many of these pictures are what we would call genre paintings, showing people engaged in various activities and giving us an interesting view of the life and times of the period.

Bird-and-flower painting. Artist unknown. Ink and color on silk, height $9^3/_8''$. Sung period, twelfth century. Munsterberg Collection, New Paltz, New York

Parakeet and Blossoming Pear Tree. By Hui Tsung. Ink and color on silk, height $9^7/_8''$. Sung period, twelfth century. Museum of ▶ Fine Arts, Boston

Another category was bird-and-flower painting, which was especially popular at the court of the Sung Emperor Hui Tsung, since he himself was a distinguished painter in this genre. Bird-and-flower pictures were usually done on the more intimate form of the album leaf, which could be square or fan-shaped, and was mounted in a book. In these pictures, the artist did not attempt to portray specific birds or flowers at a given time, but generalized from essential traits.

Nine-Dragon scroll. By Ch'en Jung. Ink on paper, height 18″.
Sung period, thirteenth century. Museum of Fine Arts, Boston

The Chinese believed that the world was inhabited by all sorts of supernatural animals, the most important being the dragon, which from ancient times was considered both auspicious and awesome in power. In the Sung classification of paintings, there was a separate category for dragons, and some of the greatest artists specialized in this genre, producing masterpieces in which the swirling forms of dragons half-obscured by clouds were magnificently portrayed.

Celadon jar with dragon decoration. Porcelain, height 9⁷/₈″. Sung period, twelfth century.
William Rockhill Nelson Gallery and Mary Atkins Museum, Kansas City

Next to painting, the most brilliant achievement of the Sung period was the ceramics, which many critics feel are the finest that have ever been produced. Certainly the beauty and sophistication of the best of the Sung

Ting plate with impressed design. Porcelain, diameter $2^1/_2''$. Sung period, twelfth century. William Rockhill Nelson Gallery and Mary Atkins Museum, Kansas City

wares made for the imperial court have never been surpassed, even in China. The porcelains in particular represent a triumph beyond that of any other civilization, combining perfect forms with colors of the rarest beauty.

Chün jar. Porcelain, height 3¹/₂″. Sung period,
twelfth century. British Museum, London

Chien tea bowl. Stoneware, height 3″. Sung period,
twelfth century. Museum of Fine Arts, Boston ▶

Sung ceramics were not limited to porcelain—in fact, some of the finest works were made in stoneware, which was preferred for certain functions, such as cups used for drinking tea, or containers for flowers. In contrast to the finished perfection of the Sung porcelains, these wares with their heavy bodies and thick glazes often have a strength which has appealed both to the Japanese tea masters and to modern potters.

Most of the Sung wares were monochromes. When decorative designs were used, they were treated in a very abstract manner, and beautifully fitted to the shape and surface of the vessel. The motifs are usually derived

from nature—flowers, leaves, birds—with only an occasional human figure. Mostly they are executed in black or incised into the glaze, but in rare instances, they are painted in colors.

Sculpture, which had been so prominent earlier, was of lesser importance during the Sung period, due to the decline of Buddhism. The preferred medium was wood, which lent itself more readily to the soft, painterly effects the Sung carvers tried to achieve. The finest of these sculptures are elegant in form and skillfully carved, but they lack something of the spiritual intensity and expressive power which had characterized the best of the earlier works.

Seated Kuan Yin. Painted wood, height 44″. Sung period, twelfth century. Morse Collection, New York

This period was not only the golden age of Chinese ceramics, it was also the high point of Korean pottery, for it was at this time, under the Koryo dynasty, that the magnificent celadon wares were produced. Even the Chinese have rarely equaled the Koryo celadons with their subtle, greenish glaze and their simple yet beautiful shapes. In their ceramics, at least, the Koreans made a unique contribution to world art.

Celadon vase with incised decoration. Porcelain, height 21″. Koryo period, twelfth century. Doksu Palace Museum, Seoul, Korea

◀ Celadon winepot. Porcelain, height 5¹/₂″. Koryo period, twelfth century. Munsterberg Collection, New Paltz, New York

Round box with inlay. Porcelain, diameter 3⁷/₈″. Koryo
period, thirteenth century. Museum of Fine Arts, Boston

A special technique developed by the Koryo potters was the use of inlay, through which they achieved charming decorative effects. Instead of painted designs, the potter used inlays of black and white clay in lovely,
often intricate, patterns. All kinds of motifs were employed, some of them quite elaborate with entire landscapes, others very simple and abstract. The favorite designs are flowers, willows, or flying birds rendered in

a very delicate manner. Among the loveliest of these Koryo period inlaid celadons are the small perfume bottles and cosmetic boxes which reflect the elegance and sophistication of Korean court life during the twelfth and thirteenth centuries. Although related to the Sung wares of China, these ceramics represent a uniquely Korean creation. Similar inlay wares made in imitation of Korean models were also produced in Japan, where they are known as Mishima ware.

Inlaid perfume bottle. Porcelain, height 1 ⅝″. Koryo period, thirteenth century. Munsterberg Collection, New Paltz, New York

Box with bird-and-flower design. Lacquer inlaid with mother-of-pearl, coral, and bronze, length 11″. Koryo period, twelfth century. Museum of East Asian Art, Cologne

Lid of the box illustrated on the facing page. Lacquer inlaid with mother-of-pearl, coral, and bronze, length 11″. Koryo period, twelfth century. Museum of East Asian Art, Cologne

The Korean artists of the Koryo period also excelled in lacquer, in which they made telling use of inlay. Their best works, which are beautifully inlaid with coral and mother-of-pearl, are among the finest lacquers in the world. The decorative motifs are similar to those in the ceramics, namely, birds, flowers, and leaves, but the effect is more striking due to the colorful patterns of black, white, and red.

JAPANESE ART UNDER ZEN INSPIRATION

With the advent of the Ashikaga rule during the Muromachi period, Japanese art again came under the influence of Chinese culture, especially of Zen Buddhism. No monument reflects the spirit of this age of aesthetic refinement more clearly than the Golden Pavilion in Kyoto, which originally was built as a country villa for Ashikaga Yoshimitsu but now is part of a Buddhist temple. Here the shogun received poets and artists, and here he himself composed verses, contemplated Chinese ink paintings, and viewed the landscape garden which surrounds this exquisite pavilion.

Garden at the Golden Pavilion. Water, rocks, and trees.
Muromachi period, fifteenth century. Rokuonji, Kyoto

◄ Golden Pavilion or Kinkakuji. Wood and shingle. Muromachi
period, late fourteenth–fifteenth century. Rokuonji, Kyoto

The centers of the cultural life of the Ashikaga period were the great Zen temples which studied and taught the new Buddhist doctrine from China, where it was known as Ch'an. The simple and severe style of these temples, as well as their symbolic rock gardens, give telling expression to the Zen principles which were to

Kannondo at Yoshunji. Wood and shingle. Muromachi period, fifteenth century. Yamaguchi City, Yamaguchi Prefecture

have such a profound and lasting influence on Japanese culture, for many Japanese art forms, such as ink painting, flower arrangement, and the tea ceremony, as well as the cult of the simple and the subdued, are the result of Zen teachings.

Rock garden at Daisenin. Rocks, sand, and shrubs. Muromachi period, fifteenth century. Daitokuji, Kyoto

Rock garden of Komyoin. Rocks, sand, and shrubs. Modern, in traditional style, built in 1939 by Shigemori Mirei. Tofukuji, Kyoto

The Zen influence has been so persistent that even modern temple gardens still reflect its spirit. Using rocks, white sand, and moss, the garden architects create designs of great beauty. The simple elements are meant to express the very essence of nature, with the rocks representing islands, the raked sand symbolizing the sea, and the moss standing for vegetation.

Ashikaga painting was also influenced by Zen Buddhism, and many of the outstanding artists were Zen monks. Closely modeled on the Chinese painting of the Late Southern Sung period, when Ch'an Buddhism exerted a great influence, it gives expression to the same mystic beliefs, and uses the same abbreviated and expressive style. Even the landscapes painted in these pictures are supposed to represent scenes in China rather than Japan.

Misty Mountain Landscape. Attributed to Soami. Ink on paper, height 51¹/₈". Muromachi period, fifteenth century. Daitokuji, Kyoto

Mountain Landscape. By Shubun. Ink and slight color on paper, height 35". Muromachi period, fifteenth century. Seattle Art Museum

Many of the themes treated by these artists were directly inspired by Zen Buddhism, and served to give visual expression to the Zen teachings. A favorite subject was the portraits of the great patriarchs, above all the founder, Bodhidharma, known as Daruma in Japan, where he was very popular. Other subjects often depicted were the abbots of the Zen temples, the two Zen-inspired friends Kanzan and Jittoku, and the monkey reaching for the reflection of the moon at the bottom of a well, which symbolizes man's preoccupation with the reflections of reality rather than with reality itself.

Misty Landscape. By Sesshu. Ink on paper, height 28″. Muromachi period, fifteenth century. Cleveland Museum of Art

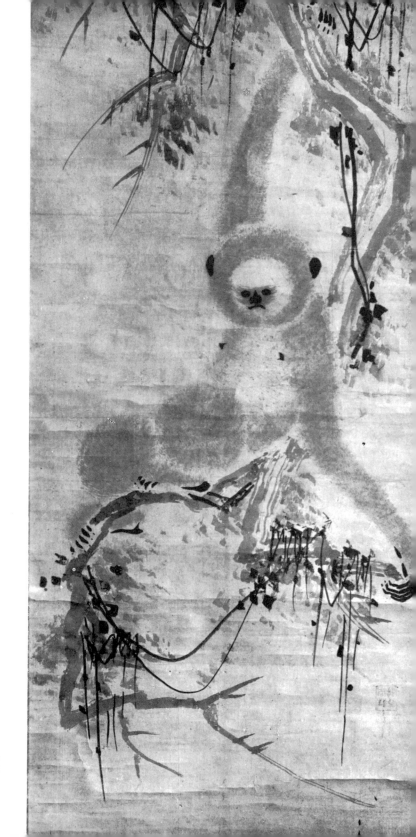

Monkey Hanging from a Branch. By Shuko. Ink on paper, height 38$\frac{1}{8}$". Muromachi period, late fifteenth century. Museum of Fine Arts, Boston

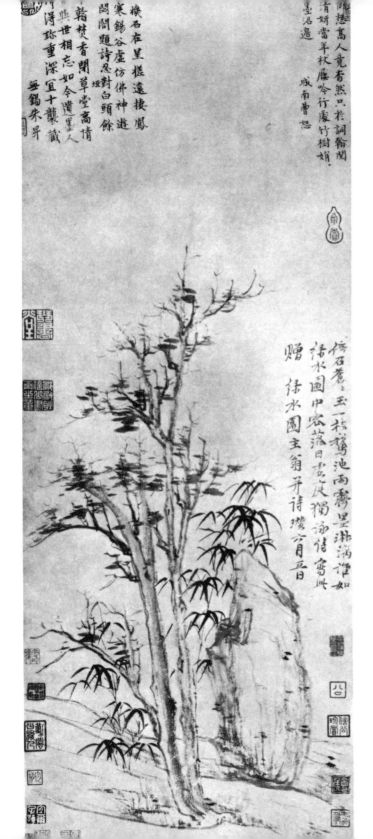

Bamboo. By Ni Tsan. Ink on paper, height 35″. Yuan period, fourteenth century. C. C. Wang Collection, New York

Although the Sung period was brilliant in its culture, politically and militarily it was a period of decline, and by the end of the thirteenth century China was conquered by the invading Mongols. Their rule, which lasted less than a hundred years, is called the Yuan period. It was not very productive in the arts, though they did make contributions to painting, the two chief types being realistic horse pictures and portraits of the Mongol rulers. Outside the court, scholar-artists painted landscapes and bamboo in an austere and abstract style. The artists in this latter group were usually gentlemen painters who had withdrawn from court life to indicate their unwillingness to serve under the hated foreign conquerors, while the former group consisted largely of professional painters who worked for the Mongol rulers.

Horses and Grooms. By Jen-Jen-fa. Ink and color on silk, height 11″. Yuan period, fourteenth century. Fogg Art Museum, Cambridge, Mass.

Scholar Playing Ch'in. Artist unknown. Ink and color on silk, height $7^7/_8''$.
Ming period, fifteenth century. Munsterberg Collection, New Paltz, New York

The advent of the native Ming dynasty, which was to rule China for some three hundred years, set off a new age of cultural florescence which was particularly remarkable for its painting and decorative arts. One of the most outstanding trends was an interest in genre painting of all types, usually executed in color and done in a realistic manner. Although not highly valued by Chinese critics, the best of these works are of very fine quality.

Female ancestral portrait. Artist unknown. Color on paper, height 52³/₈″. Ming period, sixteenth century. Munsterberg Collection, New Paltz, New York

A completely different kind of painting was produced by the literati, or scholar-artists—not professional painters—who followed in the footsteps of the great Sung and Yuan masters, using a more abstract monochrome style and depicting landscapes as their chief subject. It was this kind of painting, the so-called Southern School, which Chinese critics have always valued above all others, since its emphasis upon excellence of brushwork and its more formal nature appealed to the taste of the scholar class. The most famous of all these

Landscape with Scholars. By Shen Chou. Ink and color on paper, height 11³/₄″. Ming period, fifteenth century. Museum of Fine Arts, Boston

Ming literati painters was Shên Chou, whom Chinese critics have always considered one of the supreme masters of Chinese painting, for his work is based on the tradition of the Southern School (especially the Four Great Masters of the Yuan period), and yet at the same time has an individual style and a forceful brushwork.

Imperial yellow vase. Porcelain, height 10$^1/_2''$. Ming period, fifteenth century. Chait Galleries, New York

Ceramics also flourished during the Ming period, with magnificent porcelains of all types being produced in the great factories at Ching-tê-chên in Kiangsi, which was the center of porcelain manufacture during the Ming and Ch'ing periods. Among the most beautiful were perhaps the monochromes, especially the imperial yellow wares made for the court, which are remarkable both in color and shape. More common were the somewhat coarser, but vigorous and decorative, three-color wares, whose brilliant colors and bold designs reflect the Ming taste for splendid, sometimes rather gaudy, effect.

Three-color vase. Porcelain, height 13⅜". Ming period, sixteenth century. Musée Guimet, Paris

山川渾厚
草木華滋
庚子長夏三元
草衣為
瓻翁老先生壽
　　王翬

Mountain Landscape after Huang Kung-wang. By Wang Hui. Ink on silk, height 68$^1/_2$". Ch'ing period, dated 1660–61. Morse Collection, New York

The last great period of traditional Chinese art was the Ch'ing, during which the Manchus ruled in Peking. During the first part of their reign, that is, the second half of the seventeenth through the eighteenth century, Chinese art experienced its last flowering. The most

Mountain Landscape in the style of Wang Meng. By Wang Hui. Ink on silk, height 46³/₈″. Ch'ing period, dated 1712. Morse Collection, New York

celebrated Ch'ing artists were the famous academic painters such as the Four Wang, whose lofty mountain landscapes embodied the great tradition of the literati painting of the Southern School as practiced during Yuan and Ming times.

More original and unconventional were the Eccentric painters, mostly men who had withdrawn from court life and become recluses as a protest against the hated foreign rule. Their painting, which has particularly appealed to modern taste, is highly personal and expressive, reflecting their unorthodox character, even though the subjects they use are generally the traditional ones of the sage in a landscape, or birds and flowers. For vigor of brushwork and originality of conception, they are no doubt the most outstanding of all Chinese painters.

Landscape with Sages. By Tao Chi. Ink on paper, height 76$^1/_2''$.
Ch'ing period, seventeenth century. Museum of Fine Arts, Boston

Lotus and Small Birds. By Chu Ta. Ink on paper, width 5³/₄″. Ch'ing period, seventeenth century. C. C. Wang Collection, New York

Print from *Ten Bamboo Hall* set. Colored woodblock, height 11″. Ming period, seventeenth century. Munsterberg Collection, New Paltz, New York

The seventeenth century was the golden age of prints and illustrated books, of which the *Pictures of the Ten Bamboo Hall* and the *Repertory of Paintings from the Mustard Seed Garden* are the best known. They contained numerous woodcuts, both black-and-white and colored, which were intended to serve as models showing how to represent various pictorial motifs. Other books illustrated famous stories, chiefly ones drawn from Confucian teachings or Chinese history and legend.

Scholar at His Desk from Imperial Edicts with illustrations. Woodblock, total length 71⁷/₈″. Ch'ing period, dated 1681. New York Public Library

Blue-and-white ginger jar with prunus design. Porcelain, height 9⁷/₈″. Ch'ing period, seventeenth century. Musée Guimet, Paris

Imperial vase of *famille noire* type. Porcelain, height 9¹/₄″. Ch'ing period, seventeenth century. Petit Palais, Paris

The Ch'ing period, especially during the rule of the Emperor K'ang Hsi, was remarkable for its porcelain production: in fact, no people, including the Chinese, have ever made porcelains which are more superb technically. The most outstanding were the large imperial vases decorated in enamel colors over the glaze with designs relating to the seasons. Other fine Ch'ing wares are the blue-and-white ginger jars with a prunus pattern, which are called hawthorn jars. It was these porcelains which established the great fame of Chinese ceramics in eighteenth-century Europe.

Blue-and-white plate. Porcelain, diameter 9″. Ch'ing period, seventeenth century. Musée Guimet, Paris

Typical of Ch'ing porcelain production are the fine pieces with pure white bodies decorated in cobalt blue under the glaze. These blue-and-white wares were particularly popular in Europe, where they were often imitated. Other Ch'ing porcelains are decorated in bright enamel colors with ornamental or pictorial designs, which are often interesting for their subjects taken from Chinese history or legend.

Five-color vase. Porcelain, height 16^1/$_2$". Ch'ing period, seventeenth century. Musée Guimet, Paris

Famille rose plate with bird-and-flower design. Porcelain with enamel colors, diameter 7⁷/₈″. Ch'ing period, eighteenth century. Musée Guimet, Paris

Chinese plate made for the Dutch East India Company. Porcelain with enamel colors, diameter 15¹/₈″. Ch'ing period, eighteenth century. Musée Guimet, Paris ▶

The decorated enamelwares continued during the later eighteenth century, bird-and-flower motifs and legendary scenes being particularly common. Chinese potters also made export ware for the European market which, under the name of Lowestoft, has enjoyed great popularity among Western collectors. Although usually not as good as those made for the domestic market, these porcelains are often interesting for their designs and historical associations.

Not only porcelain but also the other decorative arts flourished during the Ch'ing period. Good-quality lacquers were produced during both the Ming and Ch'ing reigns. A great variety of techniques was used, such as painting, inlay, and carving, with results which were often very splendid.

◀ Tray with flower-and-insect design. Lacquer on wood, diameter 18 1/8″.
Ch'ing period, seventeenth century. Museum of East Asian Art, Cologne

Round box with dragon design. Lacquer on wood, diameter 6 3/4″.
Ch'ing period, eighteenth century. Herbig-Haarhaus Museum, Cologne

Ch'ing textiles and jades were also of outstanding quality, although here again the emphasis was on technical perfection rather than aesthetic values. Particularly fine are the magnificent embroidered dragon robes worn by the officials at the imperial court, which, although somewhat gaudy, are nevertheless very impressive. The jades are remarkable primarily because of their intricate carving, which reveals the great skill of the craftsmen, but stresses virtuosity rather than form and design.

Dragon robe. Silk and embroidery, length 60″. Ch'ing period, eighteenth century. Morse Collection, New York

Brush holder. Carved jade, height 6″. Ch'ing period, eighteenth century. Morse Collection, New York ▶

Hall of Annual Prayer. Wood and tiles. Ming period,
fifteenth century (restored). Temple of Heaven, Peking

Great South Gate. Stone and tiles. ▶
Yi period, c. 1400. Seoul, Korea

Although the Chinese never regarded architecture as a major art form, the best of their buildings are true works of art. Particularly imposing are the temples and palaces in Peking which, during most of this period, served as the Chinese capital. The most famous is the Hall of Annual Prayer of the Temple of Heaven, which perfectly embodies the Chinese love of order and harmony. While this is largely made of wood, other structures, notably the gates and walls, were built of stone, creating an extremely powerful and massive effect.

Korean Dancers. By Sin Yun Bok. Ink and color on paper, height 11″.
Yi period, eighteenth century. Chun Hyun-pil Collection, Korea

Boating Party. By Sin Yun Bok. Ink and color on paper, height 11″. Yi period, eighteenth century. Chun Hyun-pil Collection, Korea

Closely related to the art of Ming and Ch'ing China was the contemporary art of Korea, which was ruled by the Yi dynasty. Just as the architecture reflected Ming models, so the painting of Yi dynasty Korea is modeled on Ming painting. Most interesting is the genre painting, which, in a vivid and charming manner, depicts the life and people of the time.

Landscape painting was also important, with artists sometimes showing a strange, fantastic mountain scenery reflecting the Korean, instead of the more picturesque Chinese, landscape. Although most of the Korean paintings tend to be little more than provincial versions of the Chinese, there are some which possess a beauty of formal design which has no equivalent in contemporary Chinese painting. An outstanding example of such

Scholar's Table. Artist unknown. Color on silk, height 20″. Yi period, eighteenth century. Fogg Art Museum, Cambridge, Mass.

a work is the hand scroll in the Fogg Art Museum which represents a still life consisting of books, bottles, and flowers, resembling the kind of formal arrangement found in a composition by Cézanne or Morandi. The beauty of formal design, the feeling of order and serenity, as well as the subdued elegance of the colors, all mirror the spirit of the Confucian scholar.

The greatest achievement of the Korean artists of the Yi dynasty is the ceramics. In fact, many critics, both in the West and in Japan, value the productions of the Korean kilns of this period even more than the celebrated Koryo wares. Although somewhat crude and certainly inferior technically to the Koryo celadons, they possess a kind of strength and sturdiness which have a particular appeal to modern taste.

Wine bottle with floral design. Porcelain and white slip, height 6⅞". Yi Dynasty, sixteenth century. Hong-Kun Yi Collection, Seoul, Korea

Jar with grape-and-leaf design. Porcelain, height 12¾". ▶ Yi period, seventeenth century. National Museum of Korea

Jar with abstract floral design. Porcelain, height 10″. Yi period, eighteenth century. Sackler Collection, New York

◀ Wine bottle with grass design. Porcelain, height 9⁷/₈″. Yi period, eighteenth century. Munsterberg Collection, New Paltz, New York

The quality which modern enthusiasts for Yi wares have admired above all is the wonderfully free and spontaneous drawing, which has a freshness and expressive quality not found in the Chinese ceramics of the time. It is more akin to folk than to court art and therefore kept its vigor and excellence right into the nineteenth century, long after Korea had declined economically and politically.

THE DECORATIVE ART OF MOMOYAMA AND EDO JAPAN

In Japan the Ashikaga rule came to an end in the late sixteenth century and was followed by the brief but splendid Momoyama and the long, productive Edo period, which was the last important phase in the history of traditional Japanese art. Lasting until the mid-nineteenth century, when Japan was opened to the West, it was a period which was very productive in art of all kinds, much of which has survived to this day. If one were to select a single monument as outstanding, at least in the eyes of modern critics, it would probably be the Katsura Villa, that perfect embodiment of the genius of the Japanese architect which, in the economy of its forms and beauty of its design, is one of the supreme achievements of domestic architecture of all times.

Katsura Villa. Wood, cypress bark, and paper. Edo
period, seventeenth century. Katsura, Kyoto Prefecture

Nijo Castle. Wood, paper, and tiles. Edo period, seventeenth century. Kyoto

Garden of Nijo Castle. Rocks, water, and shrubs. Edo period, seventeenth century. Kyoto ▶

Of the palaces, the finest surviving one is probably the Nijo Palace in Kyoto, which was built as a residence for the Tokugawa shoguns, the ruling family of the Edo period. Although more lavish than the Katsura Villa, especially in its interior, which is decorated with magnificent screens, its materials, in keeping with the Japanese tradition, are basically simple, with unpainted wood, rice paper in the sliding partitions, and heavy tiles on the roof. The garden is also very fine, showing the characteristically Japanese feeling for the beauty of nature.

View of garden at Kohoan. Stone, sand, and shrubs.
Edo period, seventeenth century. Daitokuji, Kyoto

Tearoom at Shinjuan. Wood, rushes, and paper. Edo period, seventeenth century. Daito-kuji, Kyoto

The Japanese love of simple and severe architectural forms is most clearly seen in the teahouse, which provides an appropriate setting for the performance of the tea ceremony, or *cha-no-yu*, which has played such an important role in Japanese culture. Working with the simplest means, the architect achieved some of his greatest triumphs, especially in the interior, where the floor, the wooden beams, the rice paper, and the plaster of the walls create an effect of great beauty and harmony.

Cypress Tree screens. By Kano Eitoku. Color and gold leaf on paper, height $66^7/_8''$. Momoyama period, sixteenth century. Tokyo National Museum

While this type of architecture represented one aspect of the typically Japanese sensibility, there was another side which, especially during the Momoyama and early Edo period, was very prominent—that is, the cult of the gorgeous with its emphasis upon decorative splendor. This is most clearly evident in the magnificent screens which were used to decorate the palaces. Painted on a large scale with bright colors and gold leaf, they are brilliant and lavish in a way that reflects the material splendor of the period.

Hundred-Black-Crow screens. Kano school, artist unknown. Ink with lacquer and gold leaf on paper, height 62″. Edo period, seventeenth century. Seattle Art Museum

It is this type of decorative screen which, together with the *Yamato-e* narrative scroll painting, is the most uniquely Japanese contribution to the pictorial arts. Usually painted in pairs, each of which had six panels, and with the same subject in both screens, they were impressive, large-scale works, very different from the small monochrome ink paintings which had been produced by the Zen painters of the Muromachi period. The effect of dozens of such screens displayed in the palaces must have been truly magnificent.

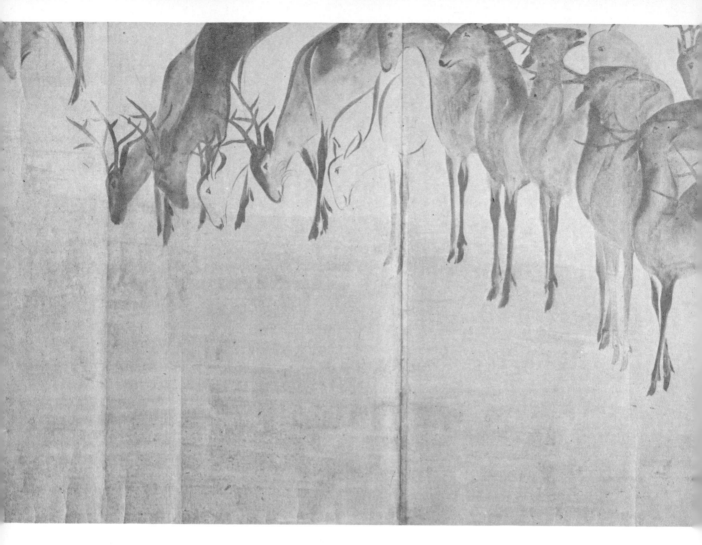

Section of *Deer* scroll. By Sotatsu. Ink, gold, and silver on paper, height 12⅝". Edo period, seventeenth century. Seattle Art Museum

Of the many outstanding painters who worked during the Edo period, the greatest and most original was no doubt Sotatsu, who exemplifies the indigenous Japanese tradition at its best. Combining the narrative with the decorative, he achieves results which are of a very high order. In contrast to the ink painters, who generally employed Chinese subjects, he and his followers usually painted scenes from Japanese life and literature, thus emphasizing that they were Japanese artists drawing upon their own native traditions. A fine example of Sotatsu's style is the *Deer* scroll in the Seattle Art Museum.

Iris screens. By Korin. Color on gold paper, height 59″.
Edo period, eighteenth century. Nezu Museum, Tokyo

Of Sotatsu's followers, the most outstanding was Korin, who is famous for his decorative screens, although, interestingly enough, he is equally celebrated for his designs for lacquer wares, kimonos, and ceramics. His style is very decorative and elegant, reflecting the spirit of eighteenth-century Japan, when something of the vigor of the Momoyama and Early Edo periods had spent itself.

Another type of Edo period painting which is typically Japanese is the *Ukiyo-e* school, which specialized in pictures of courtesans and Kabuki actors. Although originating as a type of genre painting depicting the life of Yoshiwara, the pleasure district of Edo, it became best known for its woodblock prints, which enjoyed immense popularity both in Edo period Japan and in nineteenth-century Europe and America. In fact, no other type of Japanese art has ever been as successful or exerted so much influence in the West.

Courtesan. Style of Kaigetsudo. Color on paper, height 37³/₄". Edo period, eighteenth century. Preetorius Collection, Munich

Courtesan and Servant. By Utamaro. Colored woodblock, height ▶ 14³/₈". Edo period, eighteenth century. Austrian Museum of Applied Art, Vienna

風俗美人時計

丑ノ刻　后日

哥麿筆

231

The Poet Abe no Nakamaro Contemplating the Moon. By Hokusai. Colored woodblock, height 19⁵/₈″. Edo period, nineteenth century. Private collection, New York

Drum Bridge in the Kameido Garden. By Hiroshige. ▶ Colored woodcut, height 13³/₈″. Edo period, nineteenth century. Austrian Museum of Applied Art, Vienna

While the early *Ukiyo-e* masters specialized in the human figure, the later artists, notably Hokusai and Hiroshige, both of whom were active during the first half of the nineteenth century, concentrated upon the landscape print. Their work was characteristically Japanese both in its formal qualities and its choice of subject, for they not only portrayed typical Japanese scenery such as Mount Fuji or the Tokaido Road, they also gave colorful views of contemporary Edo life.

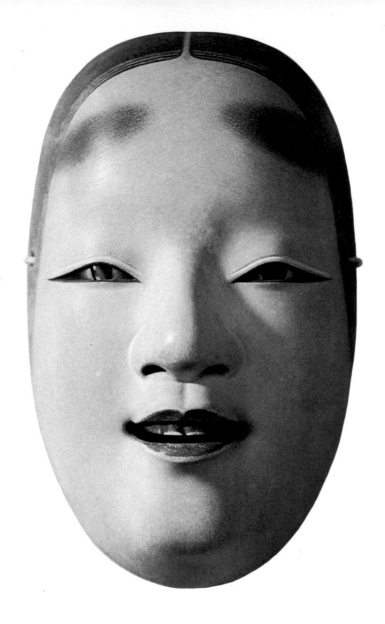

Noh mask of a beautiful woman. Painted wood, height 8¹/₂″. Edo period, eighteenth century. Munsterberg Collection, New Paltz, New York

Buddhist sculpture continued to decline during this period. The best Edo carvings are probably the wooden masks used in the *Noh* drama, which had originated during the Muromachi period and which now became very popular. Each one represents a specific type of person, such as a beautiful woman, a priest, or a demon.

Kyogen mask of humorous character. Painted wood, height 7⅝". Edo period, eighteenth century. Munsterberg Collection, New Paltz, New York

Noh costume with flower-and-carriage design. Silk, embroidery, and gold leaf appliqué. Momoyama period, sixteenth century. Teirokukai Collection, Tokyo

Noh costume with poetic calligraphy. Stiff brocade with color, length 56″. Edo period, seventeenth century. National Museum, Tokyo

The *Noh* theatre was also an important patron of the textile artists, for in addition to their masks the actors wore magnificent robes, the most outstanding of which show the inventiveness, taste, and skill of the Japanese textile workers at their best. Some of the finest Japanese kimonos were made for the *Noh* stage. The garments from the seventeenth century are especially brilliant, and the best of these are considered among the masterpieces of Japanese textile manufacture.

Among the other crafts which flourished during the Momoyama and Edo periods, the most outstanding was ceramics. The various dishes used during the tea ceremony—pots, tea containers, cups—are especially remarkable. Made of pottery rather than porcelain, they reflect the taste of the tea masters, several of whom were responsible for originating some of the best-known teawares. Particularly fine were the tea bowls with their thick glazes and strong, simple shapes. In fact, they were so highly valued by Japanese connoisseurs that the most celebrated have names of their own and today are regarded as national treasures.

Raku tea bowl. Glazed pottery, diameter $3^3/_4''$. Edo period, eighteenth century. Munsterberg Collection, New Paltz, New York

Shino tea bowl. Glazed pottery, diameter 5$^{1}/_{2}$″. Momoyama period, seventeenth century. Fogg Art Museum, Cambridge, Mass.

Other types of ceramic vessels used in the performance of *cha-no-yu* were the hot-water containers, the *chaire*, or tea caddies, in which green tea powder is kept, and the dishes on which the sweet bean-paste cakes served with the tea were offered to the guests. The finest of these were artistic creations of a very high order, and they are justly prized not only by the tea devotees, or *cha-jin*, but also by modern Western potters, who see in them an honesty and sturdiness which they greatly admire.

Grey *Shino* dish. Glazed pottery, length 9″. Momoyama period, seventeenth century. Coolidge Collection, Ipswich, Mass.

Karatsu jar. Glazed pottery, diameter 7″. Momoyama period, seventeenth century. Coolidge Collection, Ipswich, Mass.

The tea masters were also the first to appreciate the beauty of the traditional wares of rural Japan, whose unpretentious and rustic spirit greatly appealed to them. Pottery like that made at Bizen, Tamba, and Shigaraki did indeed embody the best of the native ceramic tradition, in which the effect depends entirely upon the clay and the firing without the addition of any painted ornaments or bright colors.

Shigaraki tea caddy. Glazed pottery, height 3¹/₈″. Muromachi period, sixteenth century. Munsterberg Collection, New Paltz, New York

Bizen pitcher. Pottery with ash glaze, height 10⅝″. Edo period, seventeenth century. Munsterberg Collection, New Paltz, New York

Plate with floral design. By Kenzan. Glazed pottery with painted design, diameter 5⁵/₈″. Edo period, eighteenth century. Munsterberg Collection, New Paltz, New York

The best-known of all Japanese potters was Kenzan, the brother of Korin, who was outstanding for his painted decorations which combined bold and beautiful brushwork with a sensitive feeling for design. No other Japanese potter has ever used calligraphy and pictorial design more effectively, nor achieved such a perfect relation between the design and the shape of the ceramic vessel.

Cake plate. By Kenzan. Glazed pottery with painted design, height 6³/₈″. Edo period, eighteenth century. Munsterberg Collection, New Paltz, New York

The most important technical innovation of this period was the development of fine porcelain with a pure white body and painted decorations in enamel colors. The center of porcelain manufacture was Arita in Kyushu, which had rich deposits of porcelain clay. These works are usually called *Imari* ware, since they were shipped from the port of Imari, not only to different places in Japan, but also to Europe, where they enjoyed immense popularity during the eighteenth century.

Imari decanter. Porcelain with Dutch brass, height 11³/₈″. Edo period, seventeenth century. Munsterberg Collection, New Paltz, New York

Imari plate with floral design. Porcelain, diameter 7¹/₈″. Edo period, eighteenth century. Munsterberg Collection, New Paltz, New York

While the Arita porcelains were derived from Chinese prototypes of the Late Ming and Early Ch'ing period, *Kutani* porcelains made in kilns near Kanazawa were typically Japanese in their use of somber colors and simple abstract designs. The green *Kutani* known as *Ao Kutani* was especially outstanding, and its subdued elegance appealed very much to the Japanese. A similar color scheme is used in the cloisonné, which was derived from Chinese models but was adapted to suit Japanese taste.

Ao Kutani plate. Porcelain, diameter 8¼". Edo period, seventeenth century. Munsterberg Collection, New Paltz, New York

Covered jar with floral design. Cloisonné, height 8½". Edo period, nineteenth century. Munsterberg Collection, New Paltz, New York

Writing box with grass-and-flower design. Lacquer and gold on wood, length 8³/₄″. Edo period, eighteenth century. Museum of East Asian Art, Cologne

The Edo period love for the resplendent is most apparent in the lacquers, which are decorated with beautiful ornamental designs, often executed in gold powder and with inlays of mother-of-pearl and lead. The finest of these productions are among the masterpieces of the lacquer maker's craft, with their brilliant technical proficiency, and their dazzling, often ornate, designs.

Box for incense. Lacquer and gold on wood, height 4³/₈″. Edo period, eighteenth century. Koppitz Collection, Mount Kisco, New York

252

Seto oil plate. Pottery with painted design, diameter 9½″. Edo period, nineteenth century. Munsterberg Collection, New Paltz, New York

◀ Rice container. Lacquer on wood, height 48″; diameter 11″. Edo period, nineteenth century. Koppitz Collection, Mount Kisco, New York

In addition to the works designed for the aristocracy and the rich merchants of the cities, the Edo period also produced a wealth of folk art, or *mingei*, which was made by artisans and farmers for themselves and their neighbors in the villages and small towns of rural Japan. These ordinary objects made for the common people are today rightly valued for their honest beauty and simple craftsmanship, and they enjoy a great popularity both among Japanese and Western collectors.

Traditional farmhouse. Wood, thatch, and paper. Edo period, eighteenth century. Campus of International Christian University, Tokyo

View toward the garden from inside the same house

Also beautiful are the old peasant houses of rural Japan, which were built by local carpenters without any idea of creating works of architectural merit. Here again, the very honesty of their purpose and the functional nature of their design give these buildings a character which is much admired by modern Japanese who look back with nostalgia to the beauty of preindustrial Japan.

The influence of *mingei* is very strong in much of the art of contemporary Japan. Especially the modern Japanese craftsmen, the potters, the dyers, and metal workers, find in these artifacts of old Japan an unspoiled and unselfconscious beauty which appeals greatly to their own sensibility. Potters such as Hamada and Kawai

Vase with floral design. By Hamada. Glazed pottery, height 10³/₄″ Modern, twentieth century. Munsterberg Collection, New Paltz, New York

and printmakers like Munakata are deeply influenced by the *mingei* tradition which they combine very successfully with modern artistic ideas.

257

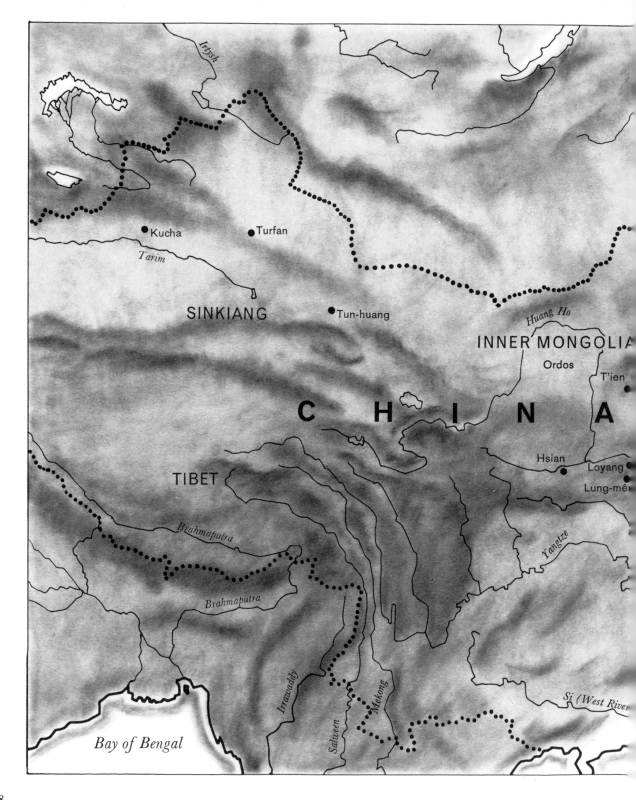

Irtysh

Kucha

Turfan

Tarim

SINKIANG

Tun-huang

Huang Ho

INNER MONGOLIA

Ordos

T'ien

C   H   I   N   A

TIBET

Hsian

Loyang

Lung-mên

Brahmaputra

Yangtze

Brahmaputra

Irrawaddy

Salween

Mekong

Si (West River)

Bay of Bengal

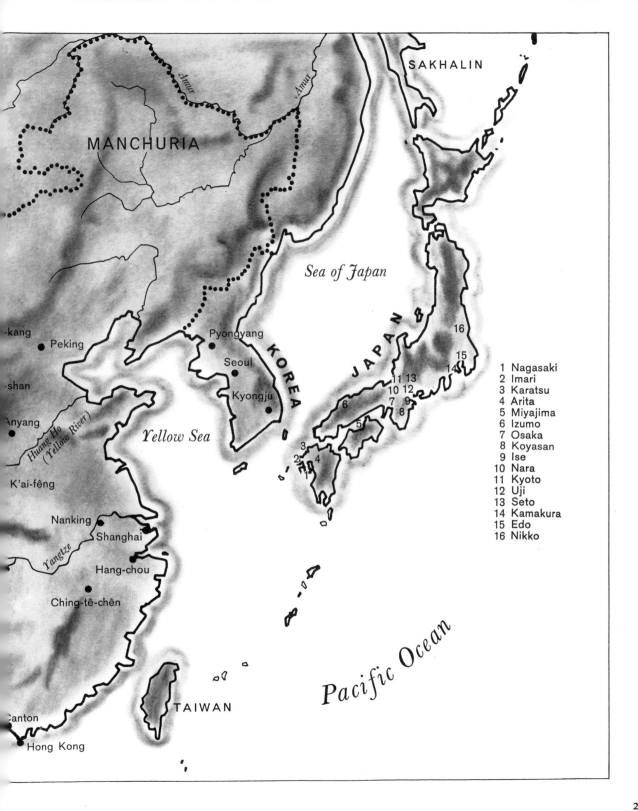

SAKHALIN

MANCHURIA

Amur

Amur

Sea of Japan

16

-kang

Peking

15

Pyongyang

14

Seoul

KOREA

Kyongju

11 13

10 12

6   7 9

8

5

J
A
P
A
N

-shan

Anyang

*Huang Ho
(Yellow River)*

Yellow Sea

K'ai-fêng

3

2
7

4

Nanking

Yangtze

Shanghai

Hang-chou

Ching-tê-chên

1 Nagasaki
2 Imari
3 Karatsu
4 Arita
5 Miyajima
6 Izumo
7 Osaka
8 Koyasan
9 Ise
10 Nara
11 Kyoto
12 Uji
13 Seto
14 Kamakura
15 Edo
16 Nikko

Pacific Ocean

TAIWAN

Canton

Hong Kong

Bibliography

GENERAL SURVEYS OF FAR EASTERN ART

KÜMMEL, O., *Die Kunst Chinas, Japans und Koreas,* Potsdam, 1929
LEE, S. E., *A History of Far Eastern Art,* New York, 1964
SECKEL, D., *Einführung in die Kunst Ostasiens,* Munich, 1960
SPEISER, W., *Die Kunst Ostasiens,* Berlin, 1946
SWANN, P. C., *Art of China, Korea, and Japan,* London and New York, 1963

GENERAL HISTORIES OF CHINESE ART

BACHHOFER, L., *A Short History of Chinese Art,* New York, 1946
GROUSSET, R., *Chinese Art and Culture,* New York, 1959
LION-GOLDSCHMIDT, D., et al., *Chinese Art,* New York, 1960–65, 4 vols.
MUNSTERBERG, H., *A Short History of Chinese Art,* New York, 1949
SICKMAN, L., and SOPER, A., *The Art and Architecture of China,* Baltimore, 1956
SPEISER, W., *The Art of China: Spirit and Society,* New York, 1960
SULLIVAN, M., *An Introduction to Chinese Art,* Berkeley, Calif., 1961
WILLETS, W., *Chinese Art,* Harmondsworth, 1958, 2 vols.

ANCIENT CHINESE BRONZES AND JADES

CHÊNG TÊ-K'UN, *Archaeology in China,* Cambridge, 1959–63, 3 vols.
CONSTEN, E., *Das Alte China,* Stuttgart, 1958
HENTZE, K., *Die Sakralbronzen und ihre Bedeutung in der Frühchinesischen Kultur* (Studien zur Frühchinesischen Kulturgeschichte I), Antwerp, 1941, 2 vols.
HENTZE, K., *Frühchinesische Bronzen und Kultdarstellungen,* Antwerp, 1937
KARLGREN, B., *A Catalogue of the Chinese Bronzes in the Alfred E. Pillsbury Collection,* Minneapolis, 1952
LAUFER, B., *Jade: A Study in Chinese Archaeology and Religion,* Chicago, 1912
LOEHR, M., *Relics of Ancient China, from the Collection of Dr. Paul Singer,* New York, 1962
MIZUNO, S., *Bronzes and Jades of Ancient China,* Tokyo, 1959
SALMONY, A., *Archaic Chinese Jades from the Edward and Louise B. Sonnenschein Collection,* Chicago, 1952
WATERBURY, F., *Early Chinese Symbols and Literature: Vestiges and Speculations...,* New York, 1942
WATSON, W., *Ancient Chinese Bronzes,* Rutland, Vt., 1962

CHINESE PAINTING

CAHILL, J. F., *Chinese Painting,* Cleveland, 1960
COHN, W., *Chinese Painting,* New York, 1948
GRAY, B., *Buddhist Cave Paintings at Tun-Huang,* Chicago, 1959
GULIK, R. H. VAN, *Chinese Pictorial Art as Viewed by the Connoisseur,* Rome, 1958
MUNSTERBERG, H., *The Landscape Painting of China and Japan,* Rutland, Vt., 1955
SILVA, A. DE, *The Art of Chinese Landscape Painting,* New York, 1967
SIRÉN, O., *Chinese Painting: Leading Masters and Principles,* New York, 1956–58, 7 vols.
SWANN, P. C., *Chinese Painting,* Paris, 1958
WALEY, A., *An Introduction to the Study of Chinese Painting,* London, 1923

CHINESE SCULPTURE

ASHTON, L., *An Introduction to the Study of Chinese Sculpture,* London, 1924
FISCHER, O., *Chinesische Plastik,* Munich, 1948
MIZUNO, S., *Bronze and Stone Sculpture of China from the Yin to the T'ang Dynasty,* Tokyo, 1960
MUNSTERBERG, H., *Chinese Buddhist Bronzes,* Rutland, Vt., 1967
MUNSTERBERG, H., *The Art of the Chinese Sculptor,* Rutland, Vt., 1960
SIRÉN, O., *Chinese Sculpture from the Fifth to the Fourteenth Century,* London, 1925, 4 vols.
SOPER, A. C., *Literary Evidence for Early Buddhist Art in China* (Artibus Asiae, Supplementum, 19), Ascona, Ticino, 1959

CHINESE ARCHITECTURE

BOERSCHMANN, E., *Chinesische Architektur,* Berlin, 1925
BOERSCHMANN, E., *Pagoden* (*Die Baukunst und Religiöse Kultur der Chinesen,* Vol. III), Berlin and Leipzig, 1931
BOYD, A. C. H., *Chinese Architecture and Town Planning, 1500 B.C.–A.D. 1911,* Chicago, 1963
PRIP-MØLLER, J., *Chinese Buddhist Monasteries: Their Plan and Its Function...,* Copenhagen and London, 1937
SIRÉN, O., *Architecture* (*A History of Early Chinese Art,* Vol. IV), London, 1930
SIRÉN, O., *Gardens of China,* New York, 1949

CHINESE CERAMICS AND OTHER CRAFTS

FEDDERSEN, M., *Chinese Decorative Art: A Handbook for Collectors and Connoisseurs,* London, 1961

GARNER, H. M., *Oriental Blue and White,* New York, 1954

GOMPERTZ, G. ST. G. M., *Chinese Celadon Wares,* New York, 1957

GRAY, B., *Early Chinese Pottery and Porcelain,* New York, 1953

HOBSON, R. L., *Chinese Pottery and Porcelain: An Account of the Potter's Art . . . ,* London, 1915, 2 vols.

HONEY, W. B., *The Ceramic Art of China, and Other Countries of the Far East,* London, 1945

JENYNS, S., *Later Chinese Porcelain: The Ch'ing Dynasty (1644-1912),* 2nd ed., London, 1959

JENYNS, S., *Ming Pottery and Porcelain,* London, 1953

SPEISER, W., *Die Lackkunst in Ostasien,* Baden-Baden, 1965

ZIMMERMANN, E., *Chinesisches Porzellan und die Übrigen Keramischen Erzeugnisse Chinas,* 2nd ed., Leipzig, 1923, 2 vols.

GENERAL HISTORIES OF JAPANESE ART

MINAMOTO, H., *An Illustrated History of Japanese Art,* Kyoto, 1935

MUNSTERBERG, H., *The Arts of Japan: An Illustrated History,* Rutland, Vt., 1957

NOMA, S., *The Arts of Japan, Ancient and Medieval,* Tokyo, 1965-67, 2 vols.

Pageant of Japanese Art (ed. by staff members of the Tokyo National Museum), Tokyo, 1952-54, 6 vols.

PAINE, R. T., and SOPER, A., *The Art and Architecture of Japan,* 2nd ed., Baltimore, 1960

SWANN, P. C., *The Art of Japan: From the Jomon to the Tokugawa Period,* New York, 1966

TSUDA, N., *Handbook of Japanese Art,* Tokyo, 1935

WARNER, L., *The Enduring Art of Japan,* Cambridge, Mass., 1952

YASHIRO, Y., *2000 Years of Japanese Art,* New York, 1958

JAPANESE PAINTING AND PRINTS

AKIYAMA, T., *Japanese Painting,* Cleveland, 1961

BINYON, L., and SEXTON, J. J. O'B., *Japanese Color Prints,* ed. by B. Gray, 2nd ed., Boston, Mass., 1960

ELISSÉEFF, S., and MATSUSHITA, T., *Japan: Ancient Buddhist Paintings* (U.N.E.S.C.O. World Art Series), Greenwich, Conn., 1959

FICKE, A. D., *Chats on Japanese Prints,* Rutland, Vt., 1958

HILLIER, J. R., *Japanese Masters of the Colour Print: A Great Heritage of Oriental Art,* London, 1954

LANE, R. D., *Masters of the Japanese Print: Their World and Their Work,* Garden City, N. Y., 1962

MICHENER, J. A., *Japanese Prints: From the Early Masters to the Modern,* Rutland, Vt., 1959

MORIYA, K., *Die Japanische Malerei,* Wiesbaden, 1953

MUNSTERBERG, H., *The Landscape Painting of China and Japan,* Rutland, Vt., 1955

NARAZAKI, M., *The Japanese Print: Its Evolution and Essence,* Tokyo, 1966

SECKEL, D., *Emakimono: The Art of the Japanese Painted Hand-Scroll,* New York, 1959

TODA, K., *Japanese Scroll Painting,* Chicago, 1935

JAPANESE SCULPTURE

KIDDER, J. E., *Early Japanese Art: The Great Tombs and Treasures,* Princeton, 1964

KIDDER, J. E., *Masterpieces of Japanese Sculpture,* Rutland, Vt., 1961

KUNO, T., ed., *A Guide to Japanese Sculpture,* Tokyo, 1963

WARNER, L., *The Craft of the Japanese Sculptor,* New York, 1936

WATSON, W., *Sculpture of Japan from the Fifth to the Fifteenth Century,* New York, 1960

JAPANESE ARCHITECTURE AND GARDENS

BLASER, W., *Classical Dwelling Houses in Japan,* Teufen, Aargau, 1958

BLASER, W., *Japanese Temples and Teahouses,* New York, 1957

HORIGUCHI, S., *Tradition of the Japanese Garden,* Honolulu, 1963

KIDDER, J. E., *Japanese Temples: Sculpture, Paintings, Gardens, and Architecture,* New York, 1967

KUCK, L. E., *The Art of Japanese Gardens,* New York, 1941

KULTERMANN, U., *New Japanese Architecture,* rev. ed., New York, 1967

SADLER, A. L., *A Short History of Japanese Architecture,* Rutland, Vt., 1963

YOSHIDA, T., *Japanese House and Garden,* New York, 1957

YOSHIDA, T., *Japanische Architektur,* Tübingen, 1952

JAPANESE CRAFTS

CASAL, U. A., *Japanese Art Lacquers,* Tokyo, 1961

FEDDERSEN, M., *Japanese Decorative Art: A Handbook for Collectors and Connoisseurs,* London, 1962

HERBERTS, K., *Oriental Lacquer: Art and Technique,* New York, 1963

JENYNS, S., *Japanese Porcelain,* New York, 1965

LEE, S. E., *Japanese Decorative Style,* Cleveland, 1961

MINNICH, H. B., *Japanese Costume and the Makers of Its Elegant Tradition,* Rutland, Vt., 1963

MITSUOKA, T., *Ceramic Art of Japan,* rev. ed., Tokyo, 1953

MUNSTERBERG, H., *Mingei: Folk Arts of Old Japan,* New York, 1965

MUNSTERBERG, H., *The Ceramic Art of Japan,* Rutland, Vt., 1964

MUNSTERBERG, H., *The Folk Arts of Japan,* Rutland, Vt., 1958

KOREAN ART

ECKARDT, A., *A History of Korean Art,* London, Leipzig, 1929

GOMPERTZ, G. ST. G. M., *Korean Celadon and Other Wares of the Koryo Period,* New York, 1963

GRISWOLD, A. B., et al., *The Art of Burma, Korea, Tibet,* New York, 1964

HONEY, W. B., *Corean Pottery,* New York, 1947

KIM, C., and KIM, W.-Y., *Treasures of Korean Art: 2000 Years of Ceramics, Sculpture, and Jeweled Arts,* New York, 1966

MCCUNE, E., *The Arts of Korea: An Illustrated History,* Rutland, Vt., 1962

ART OF THE STEPPES

BOROVKA, G. I., *Scythian Art,* London, 1928

JETTMAR, K., *Art of the Steppes,* New York, 1967

RICE, T. T., *The Scythians,* New York, 1957

ROSTOVTSEV, M. J., *The Animal Style in South Russia and China,* Princeton, 1929

ART OF CENTRAL ASIA

BUSSAGLI, M., *Painting of Central Asia,* Cleveland, 1963

LE COQ, A. VON, *Buried Treasures of Chinese Turkestan,* London, 1928

LE COQ, A. VON, and WALDSCHMIDT, E., *Die Buddhistische Spätantike in Mittelasien,* Berlin, 1922–33, 7 vols.

RICE, T. T., *The Ancient Arts of Central Asia,* New York, 1965

Index